T0078268

Bamboo Theory

Bamboo Theory

Common Sense, isn't it?

Ivan Miranda

PARTRIDGE

A Penguin Random House Company

To order additional copies of this book, contact
Partridge India
000 800 10062 62
orders.india@partridgepublishing.com

www.partridgepublishing.com/india

CONTENTS

To my wife, to JBIMS, to my family,
and to all my dear friends …

PREFACE

During my MBA days at Jamnalal Bajaj Institute of Management Studies (JBIMS), I was also employed with an MNC, which was a 'back office operations' unit. I came across varied management concepts, problems at work, politics at work, personalities, food at the canteen (*Misal Pav* being my favorite snack), emotions, books, webpages, etc. It was an interesting time as I was able to relate to what I had learned and apply them at work. I always liked the idea of having a fusion of different things, just like the *Misal Pav* did, and these three years gave me that.

I can humbly say that those three years changed my life for better, and this book is a *Misal* (fusion) of acknowledgments, summary of all the theories/concepts I learned, what I enjoyed and what I experienced during those three years.

This work would not have been possible without the support of the following:

a. Firstly, I would like to thank JBIMS for shortlisting me for the MBA program. Most contents in this book were prepared as part of a yearlong project in the last semester of my MBA course here.

b. Prof. Boman Moradian, who enlightened me with various management concepts, real-life application of these concepts and also guided me throughout the project work. The title of the book *"Bamboo* Theory" is inspired from one of his famous quotes, this being my favorite.

c. Harshali, Tija and Merra who edited and tolerated my grammatical deficiencies ☺

d. Nokia E63 Mobile phone and Western Railway, this is where I used to pen down my thoughts

e. Lloyd D'sa who designed the cover page of the book in spite of his highly busy schedule in London (To put things in perspective, 'highly busy schedule' in London = 'Half day' in India☺)

f. All my friends who read the initial manuscript and encouraged me to publish this book.

INTRODUCTION

A lot of readers (including me ☺) often skip the introduction section while reading any book. If you are one of those—Honestly, it will not make much of a difference to you, if you skip it this time too. However I would recommend you not to … and if you are still reading ☺, this introduction would provide you with some clarity on the below;

- ✓ What exactly is this misal (fusion) of content in this book?
- ✓ Who will enjoy the book?
- ✓ Secret about the characters in the book

What exactly is this *misal*?

I must admit that the contents in the book, the stories, jokes, the language used is not an original idea (of course some content is!!!). However, I would say that it is an original *misal* (mixture) of several things I learned, read, observed and experienced over a period of three years in college. So, what you can expect from this book is...

- ✓ A love story
- ✓ Thriller Drama at work
- ✓ Mixture of various management concepts like Six Sigma, Kanban, TOC, brainstorming, Lean, etc. I prefer calling this fusion (misal) as ***"Bamboo* Theory"**
- ✓ Application of *"Bamboo* Theory" in real life

Who will enjoy this book?

Answer the below list of question in "YES" or "NO"

- ✓ Is this your first Novel?
- ✓ Are you the one who has read books, that too few days (in some case 'hours') before the exams? ☺
- ✓ Are you a victim of office politics?

✓ Are you working in a back-office or in an operations setup?

✓ Is your team or your department at work suffering with a problem and are you looking for some solution?

✓ Are you an avid reader?

✓ You like reading self-help books?

✓ Do you enjoy criticizing or pointing out grammatical errors?☺

If your answer is "YES" for any of the questions, you will certainly enjoy this book.

Secret about the characters used in the book?

I had to say this ☺

All stories are a work of fiction. The **characters do not exist**, except in the mind of the author (especially the protagonist… its not me ☺). Any resemblance to persons, living or dead, is purely coincidental.

The accuracy and completeness of the information provided herein, and opinions stated herein are not guaranteed or warranted to produce any particular results, and the advice and strategies, contained herein may not be suitable for every individual. The author shall not be liable for any loss incurred as a consequence of the use and application, directly or indirectly, of any information presented in this work. This publication is designed to provide accuracy in regard to the subject matter covered. The author has used his efforts in preparing this book.

Happy Reading!!!

CHAPTER 1

Bad Start

"Rochelle, when it rains this place gets so beautiful…" I pause, and I romantically look into Rochelle's eyes and ask, "Do you think so?"

She closes her eyes slowly and says, "I do."

"These raindrops are so pure, just like my feelings for you," I say and again look into her eyes. I could feel her heart beat faster, and before she could say something, I ask again, "Don't you think so?"

She closes her eyes again and says, "Yes, I do."

Just as I set myself to propose her with those golden words, "I love you … do you love me?" A strong wind with lots of rainwater splashes on my face. "Woohhhhh shit!!!" I shout.

"Get up you lazy bum," my mom roars.

"Rochelle …" I murmur realizing that it was just a dream, "Who Rochelle???" my extra possessive, detective mom asks

"Nothing mom," I say as I look at my watch, "Oh God!!! It's 7:05… and I am butchered now. I had to reach office by 6:30 AM for a service review meeting with the sending locations (Singapore Branch i.e. by definition our customers) today. It was the second time I would be attending this meeting (supposedly), but that's not gonna happen now," I tell myself.

Nevertheless, I try to get ready as fast as possible (as usual I try to be quick but all in vain). But something or the other has to go wrong when you are late. Not a single pair of my trousers is ironed, nor am I able to find the ones I wore the day before. Irritation levels start to rise. I go to the loo, the best place to relax (I call it a power relax). Being there helps me calm down…and also stimulates my thought process—my thinking room☺

But today all I could think about was the 'review call'. Last month the number of items reported by the sending locations, in the so called 'quality log' (an excel spreadsheet wherein the sending locations post the errors we made while processing their transactions) was 120 (which should ideally be zero). And here I am relaxing in my thinking room, whereas Ajit (my manager) is bearing the brunt. I still remember the sarcastic comment passed by Ajit when I was given the responsibility of managing 'document scrutiny' team for our clients from Singapore Branch. "Have fun ... I am out of those calls, and it's your baby now." On assuming the position the next day, the first thing I had to do was to attend a meeting to defend 87 items on the quality log. The way the sending locations took me left right and center that day… made me realize that this 'baby'… as referred to by Ajit… was actually a mischievous one and managing it would be a tough jobL

But then looking at the positives of getting up late… based on my last experience of the review meeting (no less than hell) I thought, defending my absence to Ajit would be any day simpler than having to face those guys from the sending locations. Finally, I found a pair of trousers…neatly ironed… in the toilet (kept wondering how the hell it came there). The next twenty minutes, it was all chaos, I kept shouting… so did my mom… and my dad trying to explain (in vain) how efficiently the Japanese get ready (for work). And finally… I'm all set to leave for office.

"Good Morning Alban." I hear a sweet voice as I enter the office elevator. Ohh… It's Rochelle my college friend (my dream girl☺). The most beautiful girl in our college… Her beautiful eyes… that cute smile…aah…made me fall for her, the moment I saw her in college. We would have had kids by now, but those useless scientists, who could invent all kinds of medicines to do all kinds of stuff, but they couldn't invent something that gave little courage to people who are cool and calm like me.☹ Without the un-invented courage pill, it was absolutely impossible for me to tell her what I felt about her… and it never took off (not my fault you see☺). Sad love story… I know… but now we both are DTBites (people working for DTB i.e. Dutch Bank are called so).

"Goooooood Morninnnggggg… Mr. Thinker… What happened?? What's the matter??" Rochelle asked.

"Good morning Rochelle…Well… Nothing really… Just a bad start I guess," I replied, wondering when these random thoughts would become more systematic.

"Meeting me is a bad start!!!" Rochelle countered.

"No No No…" I immediately corrected myself and continued, "It was worst earlier, after meeting you it's bad now. So this meeting has made a positive difference… WORST … WORSE … BAD … you see?" I replied (phew).

"Wow!! What a statement!! I am so good at covering up, hope I am able to use this ultimate skill of mine with Ajit as well," I wonder☺

"Stop exaggerating!!" Pops up another thought.

"Have a nice day Mr. Thinker… I need to go to the HR, see you for lunch today." Rochelle interrupts my thoughts and me

"Ah…Okay… You have a nice day too," I reply.

"Cool!! I've got a date today," I tell myself, and blush☺

"Yeah yeah... A tube light lunch," pops up another thought.

I reach my floor, which is one big hall with around 350 workstations (but only 2 toilets ... I wonder who did this ratio analysis)… Walking from one end to the other takes around 2-3 minutes. The conference room where the call was going on is right at the other end of the floor. I walk towards my desk wondering what would be in store for me. I see that Ajit was not at his desk and before I could enquire about him, I hear a desperate voice from the adjacent desk.

"Good morning Alban… Ajit was desperately trying to call you, but your phone was switched off," Mehul said. Mehul is my colleague and had joined the bank a few months after me. We have been good friends ever since we had started working together. I am his manager now, and he plays a very crucial role in my team. He tries to be like me, and I love him for that.☺

"What was Ajit's state of mind after the meeting?" I ask him expecting an exaggerated response.

"He has not come out yet," he replies.

"The meeting was supposed to start at 7:30… right?" I cross check.

"It did start ON TIME!" he replies emphasizing the word 'ON TIME' just to make me feel guilty of being late. On hearing this, thoughts started flowing in with full force. I am now wondering, "It takes max to max an hour for the call and it's almost 2 ½ hours now…what would be happening inside that conference room??"

"I think you should go in," Mehul interrupts my thoughts.

"Hmm…" I reply and start walking towards the conference room. I'd covered a few steps, and there I see Ajit coming out from the conference room. His hair is generally well combed, but today it seemed as if the telephone speakers had blown some air along with the sound waves and messed his hair!! I wait for him… nervously.

"Good morning Alban… How you doing man?" Ajit greets me in his typical style.

I was taken by surprise with this gesture. This was the last thing I'd expected from him, at least today. Otherwise, he is a good human being. The amount of experience and knowledge he has and a down-to-earth attitude was something I admired about him. No one in the team agrees to me on this assessment, as they find him mean and hypocrite.

"What happened today? Why were you so late?" he casually asks me.

Before I could reply he answered on my behalf, "I guess you were sitting late yesterday, weren't you?"

"Hmm…" I nod and ask, "By the way, how did the 'review meeting' go?"

"Were there any chances that it would be good?" he asked and continued, "Especially, with a time lag of three days, when our turnaround time is 24 hours!!" (Turnaround time means the time taken to deliver the results to our customers)

"But we are short-staffed..." I try to defend.

"Alban... I've had enough of these excuses, let's meet at eleven ... at the moment, I desperately need some tea." He replied and left, leaving me in a pool of thoughts.

CHAPTER 2

Eye opening meeting

It's 10:55 AM, and I am trying my best to float in the pool of my thoughts … if it's not 11 soon, all the staff will cry on my dead body and comment "Oh… This is so sad … Poor chap…drowned in his own pool of thoughts" "ALBAN … !!" somebody across the floor shouted. I looked up to see, it was Mehul near Rochelle's desk (he supposedly went there to sort some official issue, but I guess, that the idiot was flirting with my potential girlfriend). He points towards Ajit, who waves his hands indicating me to come to the conference room. I look at my watch, it's 10:56. "That's not IST (Indian Standard Time)" I tell myself. I guess, even he is drowning in his pool of thoughts. I enter the room and to my surprise, Mr. Tendel, our vice president, was also sitting there (very shrewd old man). I was sweating like a pig now and wondered if I carry on like this for a few hours more and if its high tide now, it's gonna result into another 26/7 in Mumbai (Mumbai was flooded by rains on this day).

"Good Morning … Sir," I say.

"Brood Morning … Alban!" Mr. Tendel replied.

Mr. Tendel had this peculiar style of saying good morning when somebody is late 'Brood' morning. Just like the concept, 'Brunch'(late breakfast). Apparently, it is intended to make you feel very guilty about reaching late.

"Have a seat," he tells me and instructs Ajit, "Ajit… You can continue with your agenda"

"Branches are not happy with our services, 24 hours of turnaround is what we had promised them and the current cycle time is on an average 2 to 3 days," before Ajit could continue I blurted out, "it was 4-5 days earlier and I have brought it down to 2 days."

"Yeah… I know, and we really appreciate what you have done. But 2 days of cycle time is not acceptable, especially when our competitors are doing the same work in 6 hours" Ajit remarked.

Before Ajit could continue further, Mr. Tendel said, "Forget 6 hours, tell me if it is possible to deliver in 24 hours??"

There is a silence. Ajit and I are staring at each other and I guess both of us were expecting the other to respond. I finally break the silence, "Impossible!! Unless we are given additional resource."

"OKAY!! This meeting is over … It is IMPOSSIBLE to get approval for any additional resources and I guess, it's IMPOSSIBLE to hold back this process too," Mr. Tendel said in a tone similar to that of a judge in a courtroom passing a fiery judgment.

"Sorry … I didn't get you?" I try to clarify.

"The Singapore onshore team has decided to take back the process and they have given us a month's time to show improvement," Ajit replied to my query.

"SIGNIFICANT IMPROVEMENT!!" Mr. Tendel emphasizes and continues, "Since Ajit would be going on leave for his marriage, its up to you now to save this process."

It was a "Happy-Sad" kind of a moment; HAPPY as management had faith in me, and SAD because I knew, I could not do much about the current situation. Since the happiness quotient was on a higher side, I accepted it as a challenge.

"You can leave now, and I want a daily update on the status … okay??" Mr. Tendel instructs me. I left the room and after a few steps, I realize that I have left my favorite pen (which Rochelle had gifted) in the conference room, so I turn back. The room was ajar, enough to hear what was being spoken inside. Before I could go in, I overhear Ajit saying to Mr. Tendel

"We have lost it and I don't think Alban has got any managerial capacity or experience to pull this through. The way I have managed to reduce the cycle time in the last few weeks, I think I have to double my effort and for that I will have to postpone my marriage and continue working"

"WOW!! What was that???" I tell myself shockingly. For the last 2 months, Ajit was busy with his girl on the company paid phone, he had apparently sprained his neck, as well. And now here this hypocrite is taking all the credit of the improvements I had made. That would have been acceptable to some extent, however, appraising me as being incapable, that too in front of Mr. Tendel, really hurt☹

"No… You must not postpone your marriage." Mr. Tendel's comment interrupts my thought.

"Right now... I guess we have no choice, but to wait and watch how the ship sinks. Meanwhile, I'll check with the top management if they can extend it by a few more months," Mr. Tendel said.

The next thing what I heard was heart breaking (Guess it was more painful than Rochelle saying NO to me, that is if ever I managed to propose her) ... Mr. Tendel said to Ajit, "I am proud of you Ajit, don't know if I could ever get another Ajit."

I just dumped my pen there to hear all the crap on behalf of me, and walked straight to my desk. I was fuming with anger, staring at my mailbox, feeling just like a sick dog all wet in the rains, sitting next to the gutter and staring at it. I could see all the motivation going down the drain (that gutter). Felt like "IDIOT" was written in bold letters all over my face.

"ENOUGH!!" I tell myself, I can't stay here any more. I google for resignation letters and found quite a few websites on the searched content. I was about to click one of those links, when my phone rang. The display showed "......HELL ". How ironic, that's exactly the way I was feeling now. Anyway... that was Rochelle, the display of my phone was all screwed up, and was showing few characters only.

"Hey... Sweety ... What about lunch?" she asked me in a very sweet voice. I checked my watch and it was half past two, and I wondered how quickly time passes, especially when I am engrossed in my thoughts.

"Hello ... Can you hear me? Are you there?" Rochelle interrupted,

"Yeah, I'm here... Lunch... yeah... Let's go," I finally replied.

CHAPTER 3

"Date" that Initiated the Change

Felt like this was the most screwed up 'DATE' I ever had. Ten minutes of silence, Rochelle having her food, I was physically counting the ingredients in my plate, and mentally the overheard conversation between Mr. Tendel and Ajit was playing on repeat mode.

"Is everything okay Mr. Thinker??" Rochelle asks in a rather irritated tone

"Oh… yeah… hmm… Not really," I say, I was all confused.

"What happened? What's the matter with you today? In the morning too you seemed to be disturbed, and now I'm 100% sure that you are disturbed," Rochelle said.

I was silent, and my head was down, wondering something. She then held my hand—wooh hoo… adrenaline started pumping into my blood, my heartbeats rose the moment I was touched.

"Wow, such a soft hand… All my worries were slowly disappearing," I wondered. I felt as if we both were holding hands and walking on the beach

"Alban… ALBAN!" she shouted and woke me up. "What happened?" she enquired. She seemed worried now, and I could see that on her face.

"Nothing… I am just lost… Not able to understand what's happening," I said covering up my daydreaming.

"Let's go for a walk," she said still holding my hand.

Next to our office building there is a Joggers Park. Earlier, it was closed between 12 to 4 pm. But on request from the office goers and call center executives, it is now open 24 x 7. We are walking now (she left my hand already L), and it takes four complete rounds of the park for me to narrate my saga. I felt a bit better after telling her what I was going through.

"Hmm…" was what Rochelle had to say, "I guess… It's too late now. We need to get back to the floor." Just before we were to depart, she said, "Take care baby… Think twice before you take any decision. I don't know what the solution to your problem is. But one thing what I am sure of after being with you for so long is that, you'll FIGHT and won't FLIGHT and would surely emerge victoriously. And I can bet on it."

"Wow … what a motivation!" a thought bursts and we leave ☺

I am at my desk, and I was staring at the resignation formats on the screen and was randomly wondering. "It was not a bad date after all," I tell myself and pray to God, "Hey Lord, make someone invent this 'Courage Pill', please?" I close the draft of the resignation and open a blank word document and start listing down the problems I have been facing—

1. We are not processing documents on time.
2. There is a lot of work pressure on the Team.
3. Singapore Branch is going to take away the business.
4. Ajit has taken all the credit of the good work I have done.

5. Mr. Tendel has no faith in my abilities and me. He has forcibly given me the responsibility and not by choice.

Before I could think over the first point, Mehul interrupts me as usual and hands over seven tier-one (Top priority) documents for authorization, and says, "Stop your 'useless', 'non-value adding' managerial crap and finish these documents. Gene (Singapore branch manager) is continuously following up on this."

"Following up??" I'm surprised how come Gene is so polite

"Okay... okay ... She is shouting there for these transactions, and I have kept her on loudspeaker," he corrects himself.

"What do you mean by 'You have kept her on loudspeaker'???" I was a bit curious to know what exactly was happening.

"Yeah, you heard it right... The phone is on Loudspeaker... what should I do? ... She is just going on and on, nonstop, so I thought, why should we only have fun. Let others also have a snapshot of what we go through in these calls," he said.

"Oh okay," I replied.

"And moreover the way they talk, their accent, it's really funny. Hearing it is like a stress buster, provided it's on loudspeaker" Mehul added

"Enough of your stress busters, there are lots of things happening around and it has gone to the extent that Singapore Branch might take away the process from us," I told him in a very serious tone (it came out naturally anyway).

On knowing that the Business would go, his face turned sour. I guess he got scared that he would be laid off just like his other friends from his neighborhood who were working for other companies. "Tell her... Alban has started the checks and will advise the status ASAP," I instruct him.

He runs to his desk and communicates my message. Meanwhile, I was about to choose one of the documents, when I hear Mehul shouting "ALBANNN ... SHE IS ASKING ME TO DEFINE AS SOON AS POSSIBLE (ASAP)?"

"Hmm ... TELL HER 2 HRS!" I shout back.

"Why is Gene shouting so much??" I wonder. I know she is arrogant and rude like the others from the sending locations, but today she seemed to have crossed her previous records of arrogance and rudeness. Nevertheless, I check the set of documents... And I understand the basis for

Gene's reaction. 7 BHP Billiton documents (who is our Top tier 1 client), and all of them were scanned yesterday. "Six hours is the TAT agreed for BHP Billiton and we should have finished it yesterday at least, if not six hours. If we continue to give such bad service, these big ticket customers will surely switch to our competitors who have been offering better services, and sooner or later the whole centralized outsourcing unit would collapse due to lack of Business," I wonder. I add a sixth point to the problem document, "The current work load does not leave me any time to think on improvement." And I gather the whole lot of documents and go to the conference room to check those.

The room is quiet as compared to our floor, which is as good as a fish market. Checking here helps me concentrate, and I finish checking the document in less than an hour. I get back to my desk quickly and authorize these transactions. The entire process is completed within 1 ½ hour, which was less than the revised time we agreed. I open my mailbox to email Gene and let her know that I have completed the transactions. But all my plans are in vain when I see a stinker (a complaint email sent by the sending location marked to the senior management) from Gene with the references of forty 'tier one' transactions that were scanned over the last two days and were still pending for processing.

I replied to all stating, "Apologies for the delay" and stated the document references, which were completed. Before I could check which are the other pending documents, Mr. Tendel was at my desk. He gestured everybody to gather near my desk. Ray, one of my subordinates, overall a good chap, who also works hard, but has a politically oriented personality. Mehul hates him like anything... So much that he went to the extent of saying, "If the Indian Government allows one murder, Ray will be the unfortunate one." Ray on the other hand, had this typical habit of coming late for any meeting (in fact there are a few who do that on the floor) under the pretext that they are very busy in the work. So as usual Ray was acting as if he was the only guy who was working on the floor.

"RAAAY... WILL YOU STOP DOING WHATEVER YOU ARE DOING AND COME HERE RIGHT AWAY???" Mr. Tendel shouted. The whole floor stopped working as they kept looking at Mr. Tendel and Ray. Ray immediately left whatever he was doing and joined the gathered team. I looked at Mehul, a sadistic grin showed on his face☺, seemed as if he got maximum pleasure out of the whole scene. I wondered if ever I would get the same pleasure when I prove Mr. Tendel and Ajit wrong.

"STOP WHATEVER YOU ARE DOING AND ALL OF YOU'LL CHECK SINGAPORE DOCUMENTS ONLY … OTHER COUNTRIES CAN WAIT FOR NOW!!!" Mr. Tendel continued shouting.

I had never seen him in such a furious mood before… I presume the same goes for recession, as well. The remaining day goes in processing Singapore documents and by EOD (end of the day) almost all Singapore documents are processed barring few, which were scanned late.

"I guess, today is the day where everything was happening for the first time" I wondered. Just then my phone rang. It was a call from JTBIMS, a top B-school in Mumbai where I had applied for a part time MBA course. Since my entrance exam scores were very poor, I missed the merit list and couldn't enroll for the MBA program there. The lady on the other side identified herself as Mrs. Bhosle from JTBIMS. She told me that few students have cancelled their admissions and asked me whether I was interested?

"Why not ... Sure ... That is fabulous news ... First time again!" I rejoiced.

"First time??" she got a bit puzzled.

"Nothing ... What should I do next??" I asked

"Just attend lectures from tomorrow and pay your fees and submit all your certificates within 15 days," She said.

"Ohh ... That's cool," I was all excited.

"It's not cool here ... The AC is also not working... 3 staff have not turned to office ... Blah ...Blah... Blah" Mrs. Bhosle continued to share her problems for the next 15 minutes. I calmly listened to whatever she had to say... And wondered, "FIRST TIME AGAIN!!!" ☺

CHAPTER 4

Back to School ... Oops, B-School

Next day, it was the same old story. This time it was Korea and HK branches, who made noise along with Singapore, but this didn't affect my enthusiasm of getting back to school... Oops B-school, I should say, after 5 long years. I reach the Institute at around 6:40 pm, I check the prospectus again, and it showed lecture timings between 6:30 to 9:30. Wow... First day in college and I'm late as usual!!

"Ten Minutes is not too late, in fact, it does not qualify to be called late as per the Indian Standard Time," I console myself and go to the canteen to have a cup of coffee. I pay him ten bucks and instead of returning three bucks back, he gave me

three COFFEE flavored toffees and said, "Sorry…
No change". Without arguing I put those toffees
in my pocket, and I looked around to see if there
were any signboards or notice mentioning where
the lectures were going on. I ask the security guard
near the gate, "Do you know where part time MBA
lectures are going on?"

He points towards the Institute Building and says,
"There!"

"Thanks …" I scornfully say, and head straight to
the college office on the first floor to check. The
door was locked, however there was a signboard
on the door, which read, "OFFICE – TIMINGS 9
AM to 6 PM"

"Great!! What next now?" I ask myself staring at
the signboard.

"Excuse me … Are you aware where the part time
MBA classes are held?" a soft and sweet voice
asked me. I turned to see and there she was, in
pretty black salwar kameez, I could see the glitter
in her eyes right through the spectacles she was
wearing. Her skin was as smooth and fresh like
a small baby. I guess, I've fallen in love…(yet
again ☺).

"Are you aware??" she asks again.

"Hmm … yeah … the class is so beautiful …" I stammer.

"Sorry??" she tries to clarify

"Oh… nothing… actually… Even I am looking for the class," I correct myself.

"By the way, I am Heeral… Heeral Jha. But you can call me HJ," she says.

"I am Alban," I reply wondering what would be my pet name.

To add to my misery, she asked, "So, should I call you Alban?"

"Hmm yeah … but my close friends call me Al," I reply

"So Al… Let's go find the class then!" she exclaimed.

Finally, we manage to find our classroom. We are late, and the Professor had already started with her lecture. We take the last seat. I look around, and there are quite a few students present in the class. I look at the board, trying to catch up on what I had missed. There was something scribbled on the board like some numbers, some meaningless words and some diagrams. I could hardly make any sense out of it.

Its eight o clock now, I am wondering what the professor is teaching. "So Al… what's up?" pops up a thought.

"Was it necessary to lie about your pet name—AL?" I ask myself, "Nevertheless Al sounds cool … Al," I cheer myself☺. HJ, on the other hand, was writing every word the lecturer was saying, occasionally nodding her head too.

"HJ … What subject is she teaching?" I innocently murmur.

"You kidding me Al … don't tell me you don't know that she is teaching Statistics," she replies.

"Hmm … Statistics… Yeah, I know … I was just kidding," I lie again.

"It is my favorite subject," she continues.

"That's Great … I don't like statistics a bit, now at least there is someone who can teach me," I tell her.

"You are kidding me again, right?" she said and continued penning down whatever the professor spoke. The lecture went on till ten, and I was all lost. I wondered whether I am really eligible and competent enough to pursue this program.

"Guess, I need a strong coffee now," I tell myself.

"Having coffee…that too alone… is not a great idea" a thought pops up. I see HJ packing her stuff and I don't know what happened to me, and I asked her "Would you like to have a coffee?" She is taken by surprise, wondering what to say. I realized that she was going to say no as it was already late. However, I gave it a shot and put my hand in my pockets and fiddled with those coffee toffees (which the canteen guy gave) nervously, waiting for her reply. She looks at her watch, which was an indication to me that the answer would obviously be, "NO… It is too late." Before she could say anything, I remove those toffees from my pockets and offer them to her, indicating that I meant this coffee. She whole-heartedly laughs and says, "You have got a very good sense of humor," and a thought pops up "What a timing!!!" On retrospection, I thank the canteen guy for giving me those toffees, and I smile and say to myself, "Hasi toh phasi ☺!!"

CHAPTER 5

Mr. Tendel's stinker

The scene at office is very bad. My inbox is full, with queries, stinkers and follow-ups from the sending locations. On replying to one of those queries (on which Ajit was copied too), I get 'out of office' auto generated email stating,

> Hi, As I am getting married, I would not be in office for the next 25 days. Sorry to miss your messages, in case of any help kindly contact Alban D'sa.

I couldn't stop laughing after reading the out of office. "No wonder my mailbox is flooded today with so many emails!!!" I tell myself. I try to check if there are any important messages in the whole lot. There is one from Mr. Tendel and reading its subject line blows my mind off. It read, "EXCESS STAFF". My curiosity level went high at the speed of light. I open the email wondering what the contents would be. The email read as below:

Alban,

This is with reference to your statement 'we need more staff', made me go through numbers in the MIS reports and have come to the conclusion that you don't need more staff rather your team has excess staff. Refer below for calculations.

Number of staff allocated for Singapore Branch processing: **16**

Staff working on any given day: **14 (assuming two are absent)**

Number of hours staff work: **10 hours per day**

Actual number of working hours: **8 hours per day (2 hours required for lunch/tea breaks)**

Total capacity of team in working hours is 14 x 8 = **128 hours**

The entire process for one document scrutiny takes: **1 hour**

So, the capacity of the number of docs processed would be around = **128 docs.**

Current average received during the day is 90 documents i.e. **90 working hours.**

Conclusion: Your team has an excess capacity of around **38 hours (128-90) i.e. almost 4 staff.**

Let me know if my calculations are wrong, which I am sure is not the case. With the recession eroding all our profits and Singapore Branch planning to take away the Business, so if there are no process improvements, I've got no option but to lay off staff on this process. Hope to see some improvement soon, which would be the only saving grace

Cheers
Tendel

I am silent, and my mind goes blank, there are no thoughts coming to my mind. I just close my eyes, and a tear of helplessness falls☹. Mehul sees the tears in my eyes and hurriedly comes near me and puts his hand around my arms and enquires, "What's the matter Alban??"

I look at him and after a long pause I say, "Need some coffee... *yaar* (friend)"

During the break, I tell him about everything that had happened. Ajit taking all the credit of my good work... Mr. Tendel showing false confidence in me... Singapore is taking away the Business ... Excess staff... and potential lay off of all the staff if Singapore takes back the process. Mehul is also shaken especially with the last line, but pretends to be strong.

"We have to do something Alban. Can't you see we all are working without any breaks? There should be something wrong in his calculations," Mehul tries to motivate me.

"Don't think there is anything wrong in those calculations. I checked them twice, and they are correct," I say.

Again there is silence, and we both are sipping our coffee. Suddenly, I ask him, "Should we FIGHT or FLIGHT??" Don't know what struck me to ask him this.

"Hmm…" He said wondering about what I said, but before he could say something, I declare, "We would FIGI IT… FIGHT till we die!!!" I dramatize the conversation, "I cannot leave you guys and run away. Nothing is impossible."

"Yes, you are right … Absolutely!!" Mehul is also pumped up now.

"So what's next now?" Mehul enquires.

"Let us clear the 'tier one' documents and meet up at four." I tell him.

We complete the entire lot of 'tier one' documents (the motivation did help) and meet in the meeting room. "So where do we start from?" Mehul asks.

"Hmm… I'm not sure … But one thing I am sure of is… doing what we do daily, won't help our situation," I pause and then continue, "The result would be the same… we need a different approach."

"You are right," He says and continues, "I think we should start with that list of problems which the other day I referred to as a 'useless', 'non-value adding' activity."

I smile and say, "Yes, you are right, we should list down the problems first before solving them" and I start listing the problems on the board with the marker—

1. We are not processing documents on time.
2. There is a lot of work pressure on the Team.
3. Singapore Branch is going to take away the business.
4. Ajit has taken all the credit of the good work I have done.
5. Mr. Tendel has no faith in my abilities and me. He had forcibly given me the responsibility and not by choice.

"You want to add something?" I ask him.

"Hmm… We are going to lose our jobs in a month's time," He said, and I noted it down.

"Okay, now what?" he asks me.

"Logically, we should solve these problems … I guess," I reply.

"But some of the problems are very vague… Say, for example, Ajit has taken all the credit… How do we solve it?" Mehul continues, "Complain about it? And to whom? Mr. Tendel? This leads us to another problem that is Mr. Tendel not having confidence in you. So will he trust you?? … I don't think so."

Mehul was very charged up by now and continued to lash out, "You know it, I know it and even Tendelee knows it, that we are not overstaffed and the amount of hard work we put in this. What does he think of himself? Ask him to come and do what we are doing and run the show. If he manages 60% of what we do, I'll dance naked on the floor."

It was very evident now that Mehul was upset, and any further discussion would have resulted into nothing. "Hmm, I know and you are right." I replied. Disagreeing with him now would be asking for trouble. "I am getting late for college, so I need to rush. We shall discuss it tomorrow" I tell him and we disperse.

CHAPTER 6

Professor Irani—the saving grace

On my way to college, I keep my mind busy wondering what would be the next logical step to the problems I had listed. "Solving them, is what I have to do," a thought pops up.

"How and in which order?" I counter my own idea.

One thing was sure that solving all the problems in a month's time was too much to ask for. "You cannot eat the elephant in one go, one needs to eat it piece by piece" I tell myself. In the meantime, I reach the college campus. As I transpose from my imaginary world to the real world, suddenly, I start hearing a woman shouting, "AL... AL...

AL… AL." I turn to see what the commotion was all about, and to my surprise it was Heeral trying to call me.

"Holy shit!!! I am AL" I try to remind myself.

"Hey AL… didn't you hear me calling you?? … Anyways hi" she said while trying to catch her breath.

"Why are you breathing so heavily?" I asked

"I was running trying to catch up with you… I saw you at the station and called you also, but it seems you didn't hear me" she complained.

"8279088" I respond to her complaint

"What's that? Service request number for my complaint?" she countered

"It's my mobile number, give me a call next time instead of shouting" I say and we both laugh. ☺

We are sitting in the class-room waiting for the professor to come, and I am cracking some silly jokes. Suddenly some conversation grabs my attention, I overhear two students sitting in front of me, "You know, he is the best professor in this college" one said

"Yeah … I know, in fact he is the best in Mumbai!" said the other and added, "One of my friends, who was a senior here, said that he smokes cigar in class."

"What??" shouted HJ. It seems the conversation grabbed her attention, as well.

"What happened to you??" I asked her.

"How can a teacher smoke in class, he should follow some rules and etiquettes. How will students respect him..?? Blah Blah Blah…" She started with her own lecture on etiquettes. I could not hear what she was saying—As all my energies where consumed by my eyes, which saw her beautiful lips go up and down, her eyes which were lit with emotions, her face making various expressions.

"What do you think??" she asked me.

"Ahhh …" I replied, as it was my brain's turn now to consume all the energies☺. Before I could say something, the Professor came.

"What a saving grace!!!" I tell myself.

The professor was in his late 50's, had a fusion of white and gray hair, wearing a green T-Shirt with a logo of JTBIMS. He looked very healthy and had a distinguished charisma—don't know why, but even before he had spoken a single word, I concluded he would be a very good Professor

"Hi, I am Irani, and I would be teaching you all 'Production Management'," He said and looked at me. We both had an eye contact for a moment. It probably was insignificant from his perspective, but I felt a connection.

"I have been teaching here for the last 30 years, of which one year... I think in 1998, whereby I was not invited to teach..." He said and paused. I started to be a little restless now and thought, "Why is he pausing so much"

"Reasons best known to the college management," Professor Irani spoke in his rough sarcastic tone. The whole class started laughing on the cynical comment. I wondered, "A guy who has been teaching in such a premier institute for the last 30 years and had been smoking in class would definitely be damn good. Otherwise, he would have been thrown out by now."

He then removed a nice sleek case from his pocket, opened it slowly, and popped a cigar.

"Anybody has a problem with me smoking?" he asked and without waiting for a response he continued, "If you have, I really cant help it ... Please stay away from me". He smiled and lit his cigar.

Prof Irani continued with his introduction and shared some of his experiences about the institute, way back when he was a student here. He continued bringing out importance of this program, especially pursuing it through this institute and how it would change our lives for better. I wondered, "3 years is too long... Can this program help me solve the problems I am facing now, and that too in a period of one month... I doubt☹"

"So what am I going to teach you...? Of course Production Management, but what are the contents?" he asked us, but preferred to answer himself, "Since the contents would occupy one full A4 size paper, I request ... Hey wait, why should I request ... I am the teacher here... And I am the boss here ... So, I'll order you!!" he said jokingly which was followed by a roar of laughter

"So you have to take a fresh page," He continued and then paused and began searching something in his bag. I guess he had lost the sheet that had the list of topics to be covered. After a quick search in the heap of papers he carried with him, he found a small chit. It seemed to be a very old piece of paper. He opens it carefully and says, "This is a sheet that I have been carrying with me since the last 30 years, and it contains the list of topics that I would be covering." This created a lot of angst amongst the students. But I was dying to know what the topics were. "Bamboo Theory" he said and we all noted down the weird theory and waited for him to continue. There was complete silence in the class. It seemed to me as if I was watching a suspense movie.

"Ohh…" He broke his silence and continued, "I just forgot to tell you that you need to write it in a font size of 40, BOLD and CAPITALS." Everyone was wondering and whispering, trying to figure out what he meant.

"Sir … Didn't get you? Are you trying to say that this is the only topic you are going to teach us?" one of the students from the first row asked.

"BINGO!! You got it right" Mr. Irani shouted back in affirmation. "Yes, Bamboo Theory is what I am going to teach you. When I take all my work experience, people I have interacted with, lessons I have learned so far in my life and put it together in a basket—it is Bamboo Theory. More about it you'll come to know in the following lectures," he says and takes a puff of his cigar. I don't smoke, but my friends are all smokers, which evolved me into a passive smoker. Not only was I enjoying the class but also the smell of burning tobacco.

"I don't have time next month onwards, so I would be finishing my portion by this month only," He said.

"We are meeting on Friday now, but before we end this class, I want to know from you all what is the goal of a company?" he threw a question at us

"Maximizing profits," one said.

"Reducing costs," somebody said from the back.

"Increasing productivity", "increasing efficiency", "increasing sales" "Innovation", "giving value to the shareholders", "customer satisfaction" were some replies. From Prof Irani's face, it was very evident that he was expecting these answers, and he knew that we all are falling in his trap.

"Good …" Mr. Irani said and continued "But what I require, is the best answer. And that is your home assignment for today. What is the goal of a company? You all can take the company you are working for as an example."

Again there was silence. One student broke it and asked, "Are all the answers we gave now… Wrong?"

"Maybe … Maybe not" Mr. Irani added some salt to the injury. All of them were confused now, obviously including me.

"Okay... I can give you two clues." Mr. Irani provided some relief.

"A. Importance of goal - most of you here are not aware what is the purpose of existence for a company. Say, for example, you want to travel from here to Churchgate station, what will you do?" Mr. Irani asked

"I would take a cab," I replied

"And do what?" Mr. Irani questioned me again.

"I would ask him to take me to Churchgate station," I replied

"And if you don't know where you want to go then?" he questioned me again. I wondered why the hell did I reply in the first place. I could hear HJ giggling.

"Tell me ... What will you do then?" Mr. Irani repeated the question.

"Hmm... I don't know ... Guess, I would be lost" I said.

"Exactly ... Same is the situation with you guys, who are not aware of the goal." He concludes and continues, "So once you realize the importance of the goal it should be simpler for you to arrive at the correct and precise goal of the business. And the second clue is ... There is only ONE answer... ONE GOAL. Lecture is over, see you on Friday. Please don't come to the class if you have not worked on your homework," Mr. Irani says and leaves the class.

Some were discussing the assignment, some followed Mr. Irani to clarify their doubts, some were packing their stuff, and I was staring at the board. "Maybe one of the reasons for this bad state in my office would be this, all are working but no one is aware of the ultimate goal of the company. Maybe that's why we are lost like me in a taxi." I wonder

"Coffee…???" HJ broke my thought process, and it goes on my nerves when someone does it but the word "coffee" … that too spoken so softly left me with no option but to park all my problems and thoughts aside and go for a coffee.

CHAPTER 7

Goal Realization

Next day as decided, Mehul and I reach office early. We go straight to the meeting room.

"Hey buddy … Did you come up with something?" Mehul initiated the discussion.

"Hmm … Yeah sort of," I replied.

"What is it?" he seemed to be very curious.

I tell him about the assignment and make him realize the problem.

"So you mean to say that the problem we are facing today is because we are not aware of our goal?" he tries to confirm his understanding.

"Seems so," I reply.

"So let's find out what our goal is as a company and as a team," I suggest. "Let's include Pooja too," Mehul suggests.

"Makes sense… More heads, more ideas," I second his thoughts. Pooja is a fresher, just one year old in this team. However the amount of knowledge she has gained and maturity she has shown in this one year would be any day more than her seniors in the team.

"Will you go and call her?" I ask Mehul. Instead of going and calling her, he dials her extension and calls her.

"He is one big flirt, knows telephone numbers of all the girls on the floor," I say to myself. Pooja joins us soon, and I enlighten her on the problem in hand and we all start thinking what the goal could be. They all list down the same goals, which my classmates at college had listed. I remind them what Mr. Irani had said, "It is ONE common goal."

"But you told me that, he said it might be one of these goals," Mehul interrupted me.

"Hmm… Right, so maybe we should try and invalidate these goals and in that process we might reach the correct goal," I say and they both agree.

"So... first one 'Reduce cost'... If this is our goal, then we should do things to reduce the cost," I start.

"It can't be the goal, I mean even if we reduce staff i.e. reduce cost, Singapore branch is still going to take away the business, so there would be no team left," Pooja invalidates one.

"I think then it should be customer satisfaction," Mehul adds,

"Yeah, customer satisfaction seems correct... I mean for us the customer is sending locations i.e. branches like Singapore, Hong Kong... So if they are satisfied we are still in business," Pooja seconds Mehul's comments. But somehow, don't know why, I don't feel like agreeing to what they say.

"But the other day, we all did Singapore documents only. I mean the customer was happy, but still, it's not helping us sustain," I object.

"Yeah... because the next day other customers i.e., Hong Kong and Korea sending locations were not satisfied," Mehul added.

"Perfecto ... I got it!!" shouted Pooja, "Our goal is to keep ALL THE CUSTOSMER HAPPY and that too regularly."

"Heyyyy !!! ... You robbed my point ... That is exactly what I was coming up to," Mehul interrupts, and they divulge into a petty harmless argument on it, however, somehow I am still not convinced. "So… suppose all the customers are given free service regularly, they would be happy but we would shut down in a day or two… Right?" Wow! I was right, I say to myself and tap my back. Both of them look at each other. "Hmm … you're right. That should not be the goal … I knew the idea was crap … and it has to be! It has come from Pooja," Mehul comments disowning his own idea, and they both again get into an argument, which now, has started to irritate me.

"Stop it both of you … Let's make productive discussion guys!!" I say.

There is silence for some time, and I break it, "Profits!! I mean all this cost reduction, productivity, efficiency, customer satisfaction, etc. is all done to increase profits right?" I continue, "So, regular profits is what should be the core goal of the company," I say and wondered that this is what we all knew… Why discuss on it then?

Mehul interrupted my thoughts by saying. "You know Alban … My dad had started a Business some years back. We were making profits but still we were forced to shut it down."

"That would be an exception." Pooja comments.

"Not necessary Pooja… You carry on Mehul… Tell us why your dad was forced to shut it, in spite of profits," I say.

Mehul winks and continues, "See on books we were showing profits, but we had lots of bad debts. Money was not flowing, and the creditors were sitting on our heads. It continued for a few months, and finally, we were forced to shut it down."

There is silence again, and I am wondering, that if the inflow of money were more than the outflow, then Mehul's dad would not have shut his business.

"Yes I got it… I've got it …" I shout.

"What is it??" Pooja asks.

"Making money now and in future is the ultimate core goal of the business." I proclaim.

"Any disagreements??" I ask.

"Makes perfect sense Alban," Mehul seconds my thought.

Pooja is silent, I guess she is cross verifying on whether my hypothesis is correct. I let her finish it.

"Yup… It makes sense," Pooja also agrees finally.

"But … I am wondering how this discovery is going to save our Business" she says, and I wondered why didn't this come to my mind? What are we going to do about it?

Meanwhile, Mehul picks up a marker and goes to the whiteboard and says, "Assuming, we make a lot of money regularly…" He reads out the first problem, "We are not processing documents on time," and strikes the point and says, "we can't make money if we are delaying stuff … Right?"

Then reads out, "Point two, Lot of pressure on Team." And strikes this point as well and says, "If we are making lot of money, I guess we can hire more staff… Right?"

Then he reads out, "Point 3, Singapore is going to take away the business," and says, "not possible, no one kills the hen who is laying golden eggs." and crosses this point as well

"Not necessary… Fools like you do that," Pooja counters with a joke

"Yeah …whatever!!!" Mehul ignores her and continues to read out point four, "Ajit has taken all the credit for the good work I have done," he thinks for a while, I guess he is not sure how this problem is resolved, if the company is making money.

"Hmm… Hmm…" Mehul is humming, which means he was not sure what to say now.

"Maybe, if our company starts making money when Ajit is not around, I believe it will solve this problem as well," Pooja comes to his rescue.

"Howzat… Give me a five!!!" Mehul jumps. Then they both do their stupid college act … It's weird, and I can't explain it, as well.

"And what about point 5," I ask and disturb their stupid act.

Mehul continues, "Hmm … So point 5, Mr. Tendel has no faith in me. Just given me the responsibility by force and not by choice," and both, Mehul and Pooja look at me.

"What??? " I ask

"Dude… We will prove him wrong… If the business starts making money … Wont we?" Mehul asks

"So to conclude, the goal of our company is to make money, and we as individuals and as a team should focus our efforts to help our company achieve its goal," Pooja concludes and continues, "It's 9:30 now and we should get back to work."

"Yes … let's meet up at 5 after the shifts are over," I say.

We meet up again at 6, after going through the same old stuff i.e. late processing, errors, stinkers, etc. I start the meeting with some frustration, "Somehow, I feel something is missing. Agreed that the goal of the business is to make money. But this understanding did not help us a bit today. I mean, I know that I want to reach Churchgate, but not really sure how?"

"Yeah, you are right … Even I was wondering the same," Pooja seconds

"I think you should ask your professor on what's the next step," Mehul suggests.

"Oh professor… Shit!!" I say. The word professor reminds me that I have Prof. Irani's lecture today.

"I'm sorry guys… I have to leave now… I am already late," I leave the meeting and rush to college.

I reach almost 45 minutes late.

"Sorry sir …" I say, as I enter the class

"You better be… Anyway, better late than never… Go take a seat." Prof Irani says in a stern tone. HJ waves as she had blocked a seat for me, and I happily go and sit next to her.

"Hi" she says

"What did I miss?" I say, mistakenly ignoring her 'HI'

"How selfish is that … I said hi… And you!!!"

"Oh, sorry babes … HELLLO," I wish her.

"Okay …hi … Better late than never," she sarcastically comments trying to imitate Prof.

Irani, "You missed nothing. He asked about the assignment and few presented their views."

"So did anyone get it right?" I ask in curiosity.

"Nope, not a single one," she replied.

"That's excellent," I say to myself ... Guess mine would be the best answer, I wonder.

"He has asked us to work as a team and come up with the best goal for the company. He is going to end the session now," HJ said.

"End the session??" I whisper a little louder

Mr. Irani catches us chatting and says, "Yes gentleman, you!" Though I knew he was pointing towards me, but I preferred to pretend otherwise.

"Yes, you, late comer… Mr. 'Better Late than never', I am talking to you," He says and continues, "What is the goal of the company?"

"Hmm ... It is to make money… Now and in the future," I stammered. There is a pin drop silence, and it seemed everyone was digesting what I just said. Few of the scholars were shaking their heads in a classic way which meant "No way."

"Bazinga!!! … You have saved the class. That's the precise answer Mr. Late Comer. Goal of any company is to make money, not only today, but also in the future. Then only would it sustain and grow."

I raise my hand.

"Yes... You want to add something?" Prof. Irani asked.

"Not to add ... but want to ask you something," I say.

"Go ahead," Prof. Irani replies.

"Sir we... That is my team is going through a lot of problems, and I realized in the last lecture that it was the lack of goal awareness that has lead us into those problems. Today morning I realized our goal, but throughout the day this achievement of a goal realization has not at all improved our performance. The situation is still the same as before, if not worse," I say.

"I am not sure what your process is, but a great question you have asked. In today's lecture I had planned to teach you all, on how to use this goal realization to your benefit. To make what I teach more realistic, we would take ...your name??" Prof. Irani asked

"Alban ..." I respond

"You can call him AL." HJ whispers with a grin.

"Yeah… So we take Alban's problem as a case-study for discussion. EVERYBODY OKAY WITH IT???" Prof. Irani shouts in his typical style

"YES …" Replied the class in chorus.

"So Alban … Firstly tell us what your high level process is?" asked Prof. Irani

"Can I use the white-board?" I ask.

"Yes, why not," Prof. Irani agrees

I draw a flowchart, which looks like below and then I explain it.

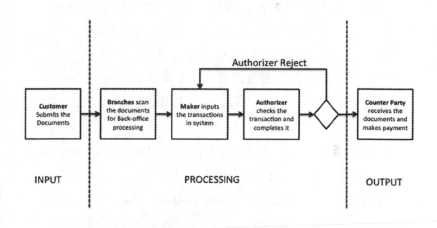

"Step 1 – Customer (Exporter) submits documents, which are eventually couriered to the importer who on receipt of the correct documents makes payment

Step 2 – These documents are then scanned by the Branches (sending locations) to us.

Step 3 – Documents are sorted and forwarded to the Scrutiny team i.e. my team

Step 4 – Makers on priority basis pick up the Documents. They check the correctness of documents and book (inputs) the bill in the system." I explain

"What do you mean by maker?" someone from the crowd asked.

"Most of the data processing centers has this control model 'MAKER CHECKER MODEL', also called the '4 eye principle', wherein one person processes (inputs/data entry) the data and the other person authorizes (checks) the data" Prof. Irani replied before I could say something.

"Carry on Alban…" he directed me and I continue to explain

"Step 5 - Checkers pick up the processed transactions and check for the correctness of documents. If correct, they authorize it. If not, the same is sent back to the customer for rectification. Step 6 - If the data processed by the maker is incorrect, then the same is given back to the makers to correct it. This process repeats until the transaction is authorized.

Step 7 - Documents are forwarded for filing.

Step 8 - On authorization branches receives a print of the covering schedule of the transaction. This then is couriered along with the documents to the overseas bank (importer's bank)

Step 9 - The overseas bank checks the documents for correctness. If accurate, they make us the payment."

"Thats all..." I take a sigh and wonder if they would have understood what I just blabbered.

"Okay... Now making money is the goal of this business... Right?" asked Prof. Irani.

"Yeah..." I respond

"So... is my assumption correct, that your company would make money only if the customers receive money, right?" he asks me again

"Yes pretty much," I agree

"What happens if the inaccurate documents are forwarded to the overseas bank?" he asked

"Hmm ... the overseas bank informs us of the error and we have to in turn tell the customer about it and we re-present the overseas bank with the revised corrected documents" I say.

"So customers are okay with it? ... I mean what's their reaction?" he asked.

"Obviously they are very upset!" I blurted

"Why are they so upset about it??" someone in the crowd shouted.

"The payment they were gonna receive is delayed by a week or so. That has an impact on their working capital," I say, "Moreover it also involves rework and additional overheads."

"In short the errors made by the checker or the maker is something that takes you away from the goal right?" Prof Irani tries to sum-up

I think for a while … Trying to understand what I just heard.

"Am I right Alban??" Prof. Irani asked again.

"Well … I guess so" I had no option but to say this.

"To conclude whatever we do, whatever process we adopt, it should help us achieve our goal i.e. make…" He said and gestured the crowd to complete the sentence, which everyone did in chorus "MAKE MONEY NOW AND FOREVER"

"And those who still insist doing an action that takes us away from the goal … What should we do about them?" Prof. Irani asked in his trademark style.

Before anybody could answer, he said, "Tell them … Join my competitor you B@#*@:d"

Everyone laughed, especially HJ, who enjoyed every bit of the session.

I was still lost in the desert of thoughts. Whatever I learned was very good and definitely would help me. But I needed something more, something that can turnaround my process into a money making machine.

"*Bamboo* Theory … We will learn more about it in this semester," Prof. Irani shouted and my attention drew.

"*Bamboo* Theory… Is this the solution to my problem?" I wonder.

"I have got a flight to catch tonight and I am already late. I would be out of town, so no lectures for the next two weeks. No assignments too, so have fun," Prof. Irani said and left the class.

"Two weeks is too late… By the time I know this theory, my process would not be there," I contemplate.

"I need to get hold of Prof. Irani," I tell myself, and I rush outside to check if Prof. Irani is still around. Luckily he was in the parking area trying to get his car out. I run towards his car.

"Sir … I want to talk to you. It's urgent … very urgent"

"I need to take a flight and I am already late for it… We can discuss when we meet next time," he requests.

"Sir… It would be too late then." I say

Looking at my desperation, he asks, "Would you mind accompanying me till the airport??"

"My pleasure sir… Why not," I say and get into his car. For the next 25 minutes, I explain him the detailed process and the problem.

"What are the improvements you did?" he asked.

"I have introduced the concept of HOT DESKING," I see a blank look on his face, so I explain, "I mean we divided the team into two shifts, and the desks were shared by the staff between the shifts, thereby resulting in a saving of almost 40% of seating cost. Which as per their calculations was a saving 100,000 EUR per year," I replied with pride.

"So did you manage to improve throughput??" he asked.

"THROUGHPUT???" I was confused and this time it was me with a blank face.

"Okay … that, in your case, is the number of documents you have processed without any errors and within the turnaround time." he explains.

"Nope… In fact after the implementation, turnaround time went for a toss, and the number of documents checked in a day has also reduced," I say.

"Hmm… " He nodded as if he knew what I was going to say.

"But I don't think it's because of this change …" I try to defend.

"And what else did you do?" he asked ignoring my justification. I have introduced a new reporting and database tool, which is better than the old one and easier also.

"Hmm… and has the throughput increased??"

"Not really," I say. This word 'throughput is getting on my nerves now.

"Is there anything else?" he asked.

"I persuaded the management for more staff i.e. fresh graduates… so less cost. I have then trained these graduates in a month's time to become productive." I said and continued, "I call them 'VIRGIN' checkers"

"So this should have helped you to increase throughput right?" he asked

"F#$KING THROUGHPUT" I wondered, but controlled my emotions from pouring out.

"Hmm … there has been no increment in the number of docs processed. In fact there are more errors that leave huge rollovers for the next day, we sit late and still my boss says we are overstaffed," I say in frustration.

"Again … I don't think it is because of this idea … Things were worse anyway," I try to justify again.

I started to doubt now, whether my ideas were really good?

"My son … whatever you have done has not improved throughput, in fact it has deteriorated," Prof. Irani interrupts my thoughts

I think for a while and wonder, "whatever I did saved some time, or reduced cost"

"Maybe the way he is measuring is incorrect," another thought pops up and I finally ask him "How do you define Throughput?"

"Good question … Throughput" he says and gestures me to note down "is the rate at which the system generates money through sales." I note it down word by word.

"Take down two more definitions," he says "Inventory and Operational Expense"

"But ours is a service center, where would inventory come into picture?" I ask him

"Don't go by names, go by the definitions. These were named considering production environment in mind." He tells me.

I nod and say warily "Okay … Please tell"

"Inventory is all the money the system has invested in purchasing items, which it intends to sell," he continued

I note it down trying to relate it to my process— moreover this definition is very different from the conventional definition of inventory i.e. WIP (Work in Process).

"And what is the last measurement," I ask

"Operational expenses," he says, "Operational expenses are all the money the system spends in order to turn inventory into throughput."

"Hmm ... but how do I relate this to my process?" I ask.

"Everything you manage in your process is covered by these measurements," he says, "just try to judge it according to the definitions."

Meanwhile, we have reached the airport. "We have reached but before we depart, I'll define one more important concept 'Bottleneck aka BOOCH'" he says, "A BOOCH is anything that limits a system from higher performance"

I note down every single word he said and ask, "Then... What next???"

"Then," he says, as he hands over his business card, "Give me a call once you have identified the BOOCH (bottleneck) and able to relate your process to the measurements I have defined. I need to rush now, or else I might miss the flight," he says and disappears into the airport lobby.

"I don't have time … Damn it!!" I shout, but no one hears me. I call HJ and ask her to keep my bag in my locker. I counter all her questions about my sudden disappearance. Nevertheless, she is all upset and hangs the phone on me.

"There are a lot of other important things to worry about," I say to myself.

"Come on!!! You love her right? … You can't be so mean," pops up a thought.

The next two hours, I am on call with her. It felt good talking to her, but two hours of nonstop chatting … made me wonder, "What did I talk? What the topic was?" Surprisingly, I remembered none.

"It was a taxing day," I say to myself and dive in my bed. For the next few hours words like 'bottleneck', 'throughput', 'goal', 'inventory', 'HJ', 'Rochelle', 'Coffee', 'Prof Irani' were all running through my mind, didn't even realize when I slept off.

CHAPTER 8

Defining Measurements

Next day we were all in the meeting room. I explain Mehul and Pooja about the importance of the goal. I tell them, "Any action that takes us away from the goal should be a taboo. We should concentrate only on those activities that help us achieve our goal."

"So for us, right now churning out documents, error free and on time would be our objective. As doing that will help business make money now and forever," Pooja adds.

"Hmm," I say, and feel good that they have digested these facts very well without any hassles.

"The next question is how do we do it?" Mehul asks.

"Two things which I could identify we should do. Firstly, prepare a complete process map and identify in it the 'value adding activities' and 'non value adding'" I say.

"How do we identify what is value add and what is not?" Mehul innocently asks.

"Anything that takes us towards our goal would be value adding and anything that takes us away would be non value add... Dumbo!" Pooja does not miss this chance.

"Correct," I say and as I see Mehul's frowned face☹, I smilingly correct myself "I did not refer to the fact that you are Dumbo, which you are not ... probably. I was referring to her earlier statement," We all laugh heartily.

"The next step we take is... Stop or control those 'non-value adding' activities," Mehul comments.

"Correct ... then we would have some more capacity and staff can concentrate on more value adding activities," I say, wondering how should I put forth those definitions given by Prof. Irani efficiently, so as to have a fruitful discussion on it

"But how do we measure our performance??" Pooja asks and makes my task simpler.

"THROUGHPUT, INVENTORY and OPERATIONAL EXPENSES," I say.

There is pin drop silence, and as they try to digest these words. Looking at their face, I continue, "Even I am not sure if it makes sense or if it will work. Yesterday, I was with professor Irani, and he made me realize that the ideas we implemented for improvement were not helping us, in fact, they were taking us away from the goal."

"But we saved a lot of money ... didn't we?" Pooja tries to clarify.

"Yeah ... But the throughput reduced," I counter.

"Hmm ..." Pooja sounds sympathetic.

"So he has given me these measurements, their definitions and asked me to relate these to my process," I say.

"So I guess we should start relating it without wasting anymore time," Pooja says.

"What are those??" Mehul asks, as if he has got the solution.

"Let's take it one by one," I suggest and both nod their heads.

"THROUGHPUT is the rate at which the system generates money through sales," I say, "but how do we relate it?"

"Sales would be number of docs processed by us," Mehul claims.

"I disagree!!!" Pooja interrupts and Mehul frowns (yet again☺).

I thought Mehul was precise in whatever he said.

"Why??" Mehul counters

"Yeah… Why Pooja? … I think Mehul is right this time," I say and wink at him

Pooja smiles and says, "As far as I remember my academics … Sales are goods sold for money … right?" she asks

"Yeah…" I say

"Assuming we process 1000 docs, do you think the customer will pay for all the 1000 docs?" she asks. I think for a while and say, "Hmm … Ideally he should."

"Our error rate is 1 % … Knowing this, you still feel the same now?" Pooja asks.

I got her point and to make her feel better, I say "Hmm… You are right… we would receive payments for transactions which are correctly processed"

"9990 docs," she says, "we would be paid for this much only"

"You are right… Sales for us would be docs that are processed error free," Mehul comments.

"So the rate at which our system processes error-free documents … is our throughput," I say, "and it should always increase."

"That was rather easy" I tell myself.

"What is the next measurement??" Mehul is charged up now.

"INVENTORY," I proclaim, "Inventory is all the money that the system has invested in purchasing things that it intends to sell after adding value."

"So what have we invested in buying that we would sell eventually?" Mehul asks.

"Before that, we should understand that these definitions are related to production setup, where things are tangible. In our industry that's not the case," I say, "In fact we should first understand what we intend to sell."

"Service" Mehul says quickly, and feels proud about it

As usual Pooja comes up with a better answer and smashes his ego by saying "Hmm ... Service of processing documents correctly J"

"Yes… You got that… in fact it is perfectly linking with the throughput too"

I could feel Mehul didn't like it, so I say, "that was a nice point you made Mehul."

He smiles and adds, "so we all are inventory right?" he says jokingly

"No … We are not, the documents that the customers submit for processing are," Pooja says.

"Why not we as employees?" Mehul asks

"Because ... We are not being sold ... The documents which are to be processed are" she says, "and by processed, I mean checked for correctness"

"I did not mean employees in literal sense," Mehul tries to bring some clarity to his view "I meant the services which we provide"

"This is confusing, but I think she is correct," I say, "What you are referring to is operational expenses."

"How are they defined now?" he asks.

"Operational expenses," I say, "is all the money the system spends in order to turn inventory into throughput"

"Hmm right … the documents received from our customers are inventory, and we process them … that is we verify its correctness and turn it into throughput," he says, and we all give each other a high five. That was a small achievement, and we enjoy the moment.

"Let's take a coffee break guys," I say, and we all go to the cafeteria.

I quickly get my coffee and return to the conference room while Mehul and Pooja were playing 'Tom and Jerry - Tom and Jerry game' i.e. they were fighting near the coffee vending machine. As I was sipping the coffee and wondering how we can relate these measurements to the goal— Mehul enters the room.

"Mehul … You remember you had asked me a question on how do we achieve our goal?" I say, scratching my stubble.

He thinks for a while, as if the computer is trying to search in a folder

"Yeah, I remember," he says.

"These measurements of 'THROUGHPUT, INVENTORY and OPERATIONAL EXPENSES', would help us achieve our goal," I try to conclude.

"How??" Mehul asks me, giving a weird look

Pooja joins us, and I update her about the small discussion we were having.

"It's simple!!" she says

Mehul's face turns red as he didn't even attempted to solve it. I was sort of enjoying this rivalry now. It was bringing the best out of them, so the devil in me consciously fostered it.

"What is it?" Mehul asks in a frustrated tone.

"ONE-We should constantly strive to increase our throughput and ..." She says and looks at us and continues, "TWO-Decrease our operational expenses and THREE-decrease the inventory... AND", she tries to emphasize on the word 'AND' expecting an obvious answer from us. However after being mute for a few seconds, a little irritated she continues, "AND the obvious result would be ...that we would make money now and forever ... isn't that our ultimate goal?" she asks a rhetorical question.

"Hmm ... it seems logically correct," I say, "but lets verify it"

"How are we going to do that??" asks Mehul with more interest to prove Pooja wrong.

"Let take some real life examples, the improvement projects we did in the last few months," I say.

"Hmm, that makes perfect sense... Let's take the six sigma one... It saved us a lot of money," Mehul suggests, as he was involved in it.

"You mean, the six sigma project on hot desking (whereby seats are shared) where we saved around 100,000 USD a year?" I ask and he nods.

"Operational expense went down as cost was saved," I say.

"But throughput went down as the documents processed were reduced," Pooja says, "and besides inventory increased i.e. the documents to be processed."

"I guess she is right, our project achieved only one aspect of the measurements," Mehul says. That is something unusual... Mehul agrees with Pooja. But I guess she was correct, and Mehul appreciated that point. We all felt better on concluding this.

"Let's get back to work now, it's late already and the branches would kill us if we sit more," I say, "So to conclude let us focus on what we have learned and realized... That is, focus on increasing throughput and reducing inventory and operational expense."

"If you don't have lectures today ... Let's meet up again after work," Pooja suggests. I have to go college, but its statistics, which is the most boring subject—its Heeral's favorite though, I wonder. After a quick cost benefit analysis I say, "Okay... Lets meet up"

CHAPTER 9

Understanding the real meaning of a Bottleneck aka BOOCH

The day is bad as usual, this new realization did motivate us again, but it did not really help in turning the fortunes around. And turning the fortunes around is what was needed at this moment. Thoughts started flowing in, I wondered if I could ever change the fortunes. I was not sure on whatever we figured out or realized so far was helping us. However, somewhere deep down at the bottom of my heart, I felt that we are going in the right direction. But the pace at which we were going, we would never reach our destination. I felt taxed out. Felt as if I am a cricketer, who is fielding since 'day one' of a test match, and it is 'day three' today—where the batsmen were hammering us all around the park☹

Pooja's call interrupts my thoughts, "What is the matter with you???" she asked, "Why the hell are you not answering my calls?"

"Nothing... I was thinking something and did not notice," I say.

"Are there some more definitions left?" she asks.

"Hmm... Not really," I say while going through the notes, which I had penned down in the car.

"Ohh... so I guess you need to call Prof. Irani then," she suggests

"Hold on!!" I say, "There is one more definition, 'Bottleneck aka BOOCH'"

"BOOCH???" she sounds confused.

"It is a slang used in Mumbai ... which means Bottleneck. Prof. Irani uses this word quite often."

"Ohh...Okay ... Let's finish it then," she says.

"Hmm, Let me check with Mehul if he is done"

I shout across cubicles "HEY MEHUL ... ARE YOU DONE"

"NO NOT YET" he shouts back "GIVE ME 10 MINS"

"Shall we meet in 10 minutes?" I ask Pooja

"Yeah, I heard the shout... Fine with me," she says.

"Ten minutes, what should I do?" I wonder.

"Coffee seems to be a good idea," a thought pops up. I go to the cafeteria, vend a coffee, and stirring it I head straight towards the meeting room.

"10 minutes of silence should help," I tell myself, as I sit back in a relaxed mode, imagining being on one of those Hawaiian beaches. I take the first sip of the coffee ... "Yuckk!!!" I spit out the coffee. "WHAT THE HELL???" I shout, "THERE IS NO SUGAR IN THIS!!"

"Then why the heck were you stirring it all the way here," a thought pops up. Non-value adding activity, I wonder☹. I threw the coffee and decided to take a quick power nap. As I was about to close my eyes... Came in Tom and Jerry, both of them were giggling this time—not a good sign for my already ruined ten minutes.

"Hey AL..." Mehul greets me, and they start giggling again.

"AL?? ... What AL?? ... Who AL?? ... and why are you calling me that way?" I try to act alien to the word AL

"C'mon AL... that's what your close friends call you ... Right??" he teasingly asks me. How the hell did he come to know about it, I wondered.

"Here your cell phone… HJ from your college had called, and she was inquiring about you," he said handing over my phone, which I had apparently left on my desk.

I take my cell and check the call log. Indeed it was HJ, and the last call summary showed 10 minutes. "10 minutes … What the hell did you talk for 10 minutes??" I asked Mehul.

"Someone is jealous!!" Pooja adds her expert comments.

"Hey don't worry AL," he says, "It won't happen again … I mean ten minutes call from your cellphone"

"What do you mean??" I ask suspecting something fishy

"I have given her my number," he says, "Sooooo… why should I tell you what I am gonna do"

"You are such an ass … you dog!" I say and frown ☹

"bhow bhow … Let's starts our discussion," he says and winks, "don't worry dude!"

"Hmm…" I helplessly say, and nod wondering that this swine had said the same thing when Rochelle had joined, and now… this ass flirts with her so much☹.

"But AL sounds cool," Pooja comments and we all start giggling. They both pull my leg for the next ten minutes, and I let that happen as the whole exercise was helping us relieve our day's stress.

"Bottleneck aka BOOCH!" I say to get their attention.'

"One more definition??" Mehul says in a lackluster tone, "do you think these 'definition solving' is gonna help... I mean to be practical, we have solved all the definition expect this one, but it has not helped us in any way... Are we all going in the right direction or just wasting time here?" He spells out his opinion. Even I was thinking in those terms sometime back except for the 'direction' part (I knew we were going in the right track). Before I could express my agreement on Mehul's opinion, Pooja speaks out, "It's too early to comment whether it's useful or not... But one thing for sure has happened to me at least... These definitions have changed my approach towards work. I think we are in the right direction."

My support is tilted towards Pooja argument now, and I say, "I think she is right, moreover we don't have an alternate solution too ... Do we?"

There is pin drop silence in the room.

"Okay … Let's try out," Mehul declares, as if he had a choice.

I read the note "Bottleneck aka BOOCH," I say, "means anything that limits a system from achieving higher performance versus its goal."

"What limits us from achieving higher performance??" Mehul asks.

Expectedly Pooja replies, "I think we should break the definition in parts, understand it, and then derive a meaning out of it. Instead of diving straight into it … What do you say Alban??"

"Yeah… It makes sense," I reply, and could feel Mehul was no longer part of this discussion. He was fidgeting with the marker, and it seemed as if he assumed the marker to be Pooja and he was torturing it.

"Something that limits the system," says Pooja, which interrupts my 'non-value adding' flow of thoughts.

"System is our process, and something is what we need to find," she continues.

"Higher performance versus goal," Mehul stands up and proclaims.

"Sorry, I didn't get you?" Pooja seems confused.

"Let me explain…" Mehul takes the charge now, "something that limits our system from processing more documents (throughput)... Which limits our system from reducing inventory (documents which are waiting to be processed) ... that also limits our system from reducing costs (operational expense)," he says.

"Yup ... Way to go Mehul," Pooja agrees, "So we need to find this unknown thing which limits our system."

"Hold wait..." I say, "As far as the inventory goes; there is hardly any which we procure. It's all the documents customer submits us, which we need to process faster. This will avoid piling of inventory" They both nod in agreement.

"As far as reducing operational expenses, we have done all we could, and I don't think there is any opportunity to reduce it further so as to achieve a turnaround," I say.

"Hmm ... you seem correct, but what point are you trying to prove?" Mehul asks.

"See, inventory and cost that we have to reduce to attain our goal is LIMITED," I say

"LIMITED?? ... In what sense?" Pooja questions.

I didn't expect Pooja to ask this. Nevertheless, I respond to her question "Limited... means... We would have to incur some operational cost and inventory. Say for example—to produce 100 units we need minimum of Rs.20 worth of inventory and operational expense. If today we are spending around 28, we can only reduce it to 20 not less than that. And as far as our process is concerned, I believe, we have reached the 20 levels"

"Hmm, that makes sense... I did not think in these terms," she honestly admitted.

"So what... my question is unanswered still!" Mehul says.

"Yes... I am coming to it," I say, "In our case, I feel we have already reduced cost and inventory. Any further reduction might lead into further decrease in throughput."

"Hmm, got your point now," Mehul says, "Moreover any further reduction in these two components is not gonna help us much"

"Here you go ... Any reduction in these two measurements would have a very miniscule impact," I say, "To make a turnaround we need to concentrate on THROUGHPUT."

"Yeah... And throughput does not have any LIMITATIONS," Pooja says.

I could see Mehul was a bit confused, but before he could ask, I add, "Yes ... technically there is no limit for increasing our throughput unless we don't have enough documents (business)"

Mehul nods now and moves a bit forward showing some interest in the discussion.

"So our focus primarily should be exploring opportunities to increase throughput," I say, "and it's so funny, that all these years we were conditioned to focus only on costs... reduction of cost. There isn't a single project or improvement made, which revolves around the scope of enhancing throughput"

"That is true for the whole department... I guess," Pooja comments

"Maybe for the whole company... Everywhere cost reduction is a key," Mehul blurts out in frustration.

"It is a key realization. Going forward we should focus more on increasing throughput," I say, "So are we all on the same page??"

"Yes...yes we are!" both yelled.

Somewhere deep down within me, I was feeling the turnaround has started. For some reason, my left-brain (logical brain) was not allowing me to accept it so soon. It wanted some facts to substantiate this discovery. Nevertheless, it's a new approach and is worth giving a try... I wonder.

"Okay… Guys how do we increase our throughput??" asks Mehul

"I think we should find out that 'SOMETHING' that limits the system from increasing our throughput," Pooja says, "I mean what limits us in processing 75 documents only and not 150 – 200?"

"So how do we go about it…??" I ask, "any idea?"

"I have got an idea," Mehul says, "You remember, I said, I would take 10 minutes more before we started this meeting?"

"Yeah, I remember… What about it?" I ask

"Actually, I was creating a process map to identify the 'value adding' and 'non-value adding' activities," Mehul says

"That's fabulous," I say.

"Thanks Mehul … I thought the discussion would get over now," Pooja appreciates his efforts. They both are now starting to gel well.

"Are they in LOVE??" a thought pops up☺.

Mehul goes towards the board and starts drawing the flowchart. It's a micro level flowchart.

"While Mehul is scribbling, I'll get a coffee for myself," I say and leave the room as the bitter taste of the sugarless coffee was still there.

"I am not scribbling… You ass!!" I heard Mehul shouting from the closed door, I smiled and went ahead to get a coffee.

I vend a coffee and on my return, the blue and red boxes on the whiteboard startle me. It seemed like a distorted 'USA flag' with some scribbling on it instead of those stars. It's a process we follow day in day out, but looking at the board, I was not able to make any sense out of it. Since Mehul had put so much of effort jotting it down, I concluded it's better to remain silent. There was quietness for some time. All of us were staring at the board—finally Pooja broke the silence and asked, "what does red and blue box signify?"

"Oh… She understood the other part of the art??" a thought pops up☺.

"Okay … Let me explain it," Mehul says and starts explaining it. Now the distorted art starts making some sense. After he is done explaining the process, he waits for our reaction.

"Mehul… You have explained all the stuff we knew but have not answered my question," Pooja blurts, "did you use the color codes to give your process map an artistic look or does it have some meaning??"

"Oh sorry … It does have a meaning" Mehul says, "The red boxes are the one's which are 'non-value adding' and the blue boxes are 'value adding' activity"

"Hmm, Are these in our control?" I ask

"Yeah, some are … but most of them are not," Mehul replies

"Guys …I guess we are going off track," Pooja interrupts, "I am not saying it is wrong to eliminate the non value adding activity … BUT…"

"But what … Go ahead," I urge her to continue.

"We are going the old way again. We should focus first on finding the bottleneck. Let us try to work on the definitions Prof Irani gave"

"Okay… That makes sense," I say, "But you guys start thinking on how we can eliminate these 'non-value adding' activities. At some point in time we would have to eliminate them"

"So here is the process map… But how do we identify a Bottleneck?" Pooja tries to bring focus on the definitions.

"All the red boxes are bottlenecks, and these boxes, as per the definition, limits the performance of our system," Mehul comments indicating the red boxes he drew.

"Hmm… Makes sense … I think he is right," Pooja comments.

"That's weird… I am sure now," I tell myself, "both of them are in love … Man, they are agreeing on each other's arguments"

"You said something?" Pooja interrupts my thought

"Was I loud?" I ask wondering how come she knew what I was thinking.

"What loud?" Mehul pokes.

"Nothing…" I say, "but then you mean to say we have quite a few bottlenecks?"

"Eight … to be more precise" Mehul adds.

"Any problem?" Pooja asks.

"Somehow this realization is not as convincing and startling as the previous ones," I say.

"But it is matching the definition given by your professor," Mehul defends.

"Hmm… Yes… But…" I say, wondering why am I getting this feeling.

"So what's next", Mehul asks.

"Hmm … Since we have found out the relationship between the definition and our process, I think we should call Prof. Irani and seek his advise on whether we are going in the right direction and what needs to be done next," Pooja replies.

"Right…" Mehul seconds Pooja again.

"Where the hell did I keep the number?" I murmur while hunting for the number.

"How irresponsible!!!" Mehul comments sarcastically. I finally find it and comment, "Here it is … Master"

I dial the number; it beeps for a while (an indication that it's an outstation call you are making) and then it rings.

"Hello Irani here…" he replied in a very heavy tone. It seems he was sleeping and apparently we have disturbed him.

"Hello sir … Alban here from JBTIMS … Sorry to disturb you," I uttered nervously.

"Who Alban??" he asked wearily.

"Sir, I am the one who accompanied you to the airport … You gave me few definitions," I try to help him remember me. I felt like banging the receiver on his head (had seen this in one of the movies, usually the memory lost gets recovered by a blow on the head).

"Ohh…ya…ya… Mr. AL," he says, and both Mehul and Pooja look at me, "I don't know why he is referring to me AL," I whisper with an artificial confused look on my face.

"Did I disturb you sir…??" I ask.

"Hmm... to be honest yeah... I haven't slept properly since I have come here. But we can talk... I had to get up to take my medicines anyway," he replied. His tone was better than before now.

"Sir... We have related all the definitions you had given to our process," I say. Then I tell him about our realizations— Throughput is the documents processed correctly... Inventory is documents that the customer submits... Operational expenses are everything that goes into converting these docs into throughput i.e. systems, people, etc ... and then I substantiate these measurements against the goal... i.e. we should focus our energies on increasing throughput and reducing inventory and operational expenses.

"That's very impressive AL!" He says, and that brings a smile on our faces.

"But sir we are losing time... We have got only two weeks now... And these realizations have made no significant improvements," I plead.

"Don't you worry Al... The way you are going... Believe me, you would not only save your process... But would make a complete turnaround," he says. "If I could save the process... that's more than enough," I tell myself

"So what about BOOCH... Bottleneck," he asks.

"Yeah we have found quite a few bottlenecks that limits our throughput"

"Ohh… is it??" he says, "and how did you arrive at them."

"We took a process map and tried to identify 'value adding' activity and 'non-value adding' activity," I say, "and all those non value adding activities are bottlenecks as they limit the throughput."

"How have you defined value added and non-value added activity??" he asks

"Anything, which helps us in converting inventory into throughput," I say, "is a value adding activity… and others non value activity."

"Then why are you doing this non value add activities in the first place!!!" he says, "These are not Bottlenecks!!!"

"These activities are necessary, as compliance checks, reporting, rectifying errors, etc." I say, "Moreover some of these are not under our control."

"Find out a way to eliminate it or automate it or if possible give it to non-bottleneck resource!" he says, rather orders

"Non-bottleneck??" I ask.

"Everything except for bottleneck is non-bottleneck," he says

"But if we have identified incorrect bottlenecks…
Then how do we find out the right one?" I ask.

"A bottleneck by nature would be something which is value adding activity as per your definition," he says, "It would be either a resource or a process"

"Some of them were processes," I try to defend.

"But they are non value adding activities," he says, "you shouldn't be doing it in the first place."

"Oh … okay," I murmur

"Remember one thing, there is only one or at the most two bottlenecks… Not more than that. And I strongly believe, in your kind of setup it should be only one" he declares.

"Hmm… Then???… What would be the next step?" I ask

"Give me a call once you have identified the bottleneck, and you are able to bring out its importance with regards to your goal successfully," he says, "bye AL"

"Bye …" I say, fumed on this approach used by Prof. Irani.

"Can't he just give us the solution," Mehul blurts out, "It would be so simpler and faster"

"I think he wants us to own this thought process," Pooja comments

"Own it?? What do you mean by that??" Mehul tries to clarify.

"It's called the Socratic's approach," she says, "Google it"

"Whatever... Spare us from your philosophy ... I guess, it would have been simpler if he would have just told us," Mehul discounts her completely

"Okay... Time out guys," I make a gesture, "And let's focus on identifying a bottleneck."

"How do we go about it??" Pooja asks.

"Hmm ... How do we measure our goal?" I ask in spite of knowing the answer, just to make it a bit more interactive.

"Throughput ... i.e. number of documents processed," Mehul replies

"So our capacity is what limits us from achieving higher throughput... isn't it?" I ask. I can now see the light at the end of the tunnel.

"But as per Mr. Tendel's email, we are an 'excess staff'!" Mehul says.

"What email??" Pooja asks

"There is an email from Mr. Tendel, which says that we have an excess capacity", I say

"Excess??? ... Has he gone bonkers" this time Pooja blurts out.

I go to the board and scribble the calculations

Number of staff allocated for Singapore: **16**

Staff working on any given day: **14 (assuming two are out of office)**

Number of hours staff work: **10 per day**

Actual number of working hours: **8 per day (2 hrs required for lunch/tea breaks)**

Total capacity of team in working hours is **14 x 8 = 128 hrs**

The whole process for one document scrutiny takes: **1 hour**

So, the capacity of the number of docs processed would be around: **128 docs.**

Current average docs received during the day is 90 documents i.e. **90 working hrs.**

Conclusion: Your team has an excess capacity of around **38 hours (128-90)** i.e. almost **four** staff.

She takes a look at the calculations, and starts scribbling something on her pad... notepad to be more precise☺.

"He seems to be right... Moreover, the capacity he is referring to, is in line with our goal... i.e. the number of documents processed," Pooja concludes.

"Yeah... I know," I second her.

"So we are stuck … I think we should call Prof. Irani," Mehul suggests.

"It's too late," I say, "I guess we should leave now… Maybe if we think over it tonight, we might arrive to some conclusion"

Meanwhile, I get an SMS… It's HJ … I open it, and it states, "hey… I got stuck with an important client meet … I would be late"

"What a romantic message ☺", I wonder and then I reply, "Okay … Evn I hv left nw … C u at d railway station."

CHAPTER 10

Identifying the Bottleneck

I am now at the Dadar railway station waiting for HJ to come.

Ten minutes passed, and I am still waiting☹. I hate every second of it. Generally, it takes me around 25 minutes to reach Dadar station, and she takes around 35 minutes. From Dadar, it takes another 15 minutes to reach college. So overall, it takes me around 40 minutes to reach college (provided I am alone!!). Usually I play games on my mobile, but the word 'bottleneck' was not allowing me to do that today. What is it that limits our performance? … What would it be? … What if there are no bottlenecks? … These were some questions that were bothering me. A sudden vibration pulls me out of those thoughts... My phone is ringing ... and it's a call from Pooja.

"Hey ... Alban here," I say trying to imitate Prof. Irani

"Hello Alban ... It's you only na?" Pooja replies with a question

"Yeah, why??" I ask with some curiosity, believing that she solved the 'bottleneck' mystery.

"What's the matter with you?? I have your number stored, and I guess even you have mine. Then what was that ... 'Hey Alban here'," she fumes, "I know you are Alban!"

"Popat (idiot)!!!" a thought pops up.

"Hmm ...okay okay ...tell me why you called?" I try to change the subject.

"Were you trying to emulate your professor??" she tries to stick to the topic

"Okay fine... I was imitating him," I say, "will you now come to the point?"

In the meanwhile a train passes by, and this is what I hear, "pooooo juk juk **I'll** juk juk juk juk **be** juk juk **late** juk juk" (dj mix of train passing by and Pooja's words)

"Hey sorry... I couldn't hear what you just said," I say, "a train was passing by"

"Ohh … I said… I would be a little late tomorrow," she replies, "By the way how come you haven't reached college yet… I remember you telling me once, that it takes only 40 minutes to reach"

"Yeah … It takes about 40 minutes … but when I am alone," I say, "not when HJ and I go together. She is always late!"

"She limits your performance," Pooja jokes, "Poor you… Take care ... See you tomorrow… hopefully we crack the bottleneck mystery," Pooja hangs up

"Okay … Bye," I say holding on the last statement she made 'she limits your performance'.

"HJ limits my performance…" I say to myself.

"Eureka !!!... What would be the throughput in this case?" I try to solve the mystery.

"I guess it should be me and HJ reaching college" I am now in an animated conversation with myself.

"I take 25 + 15 minutes… That is 25 minutes from office to Dadar and 15 minutes from Dadar to college," I tell myself, "HJ takes 35 minutes + 15 minutes"

"So HJ is a bottleneck here," I say excitedly, "she limits our performance to reach college".

"AL…AL…" I hear HJ shout.

"Why does she have to shout??" a thought pops up. I wave my hand, and it takes about 30 seconds for her to reach me.

"Sorry, I am late …" She says.

"Say something new… Miss bottleneck," I sarcastically declare.

"Bottleneck???" she shouts back defensively.

"Yeah, you are a bottleneck … and you limit my performance," I tell her excitedly without realizing that she was not aware of my realization.

"And how do I limit your performance," she asks in a bit angry tone.

"Oops… Guess you plucked the wrong strings," I say to myself☹.

"I mean, we can reach college early … If you come on time," I try to explain (obviously in vain). Before I could say anything more about my realization, she blurts out, "GET LOST!! … AND … You don't have to WAIT for me ANYMORE!"

"Arey … baby," I try to cool her down (but in vain again)

"Let it be AL … I thought you were different!" she shouts back, "ALL MEN ARE DOGS!! … Back in the office its Mayank (her boss) who bugs me … Dodo (her bro) at home irritates me … and now you … didn't expect this from you AL … thought at least you understood me and my feelings"

"Isn't she overreacting and spoiling my happy moment?" a thought comes to my mind. I let that thought remain a thought, and for the next ten minutes, I just try to calm her down. I try to explain her my about my realization, but that offends her even more.

"Conflict management is the next soft skill training I am going to attend," I tell myself. Finally, she calms down … Not due to my convincing skills … but one scoop of BELGIAN DARK CHOCOLATE ICE CREAM does the trick. And after hogging the ice cream alone without offering me even a bit, she says, "I was just kidding doggy"

"WOW!!" pops up a thought.

The next day, I am all excited to share my realization about the bottleneck with my 'rescue team'. On my way to the office, I try to figure out how to present it to them, so that they agree without any arguments. I vend a coffee and go straight to the meeting room. The floor is as silent as a meeting room. I wonder if heaven would be like this—all empty (with so many selfish and mean people around, I guess heaven is bound to be empty). I sit in the meeting room, and as I sip my coffee, I am intuitively trying to figure out what OUR system's bottleneck would be.

"Good Morning Alban… Oops, I forgot … Good Morning AL," Mehul enters with a mug of sarcasm and splashes that on my face.

"Very good morning Mehul … Oops, I forgot … you ass%^#le," I give him back☺.

"Wooh…wooh… Why are you getting mad at me dude?" He says, "that's what your close friends call you right??"

He was not getting on my nerve this time … In fact somewhere at the bottom of my heart, I was enjoying it— him teasing & and linking me with HJ. Nonetheless, I surely felt like kicking his ass.

"Good Morning AL…" Now Pooja enters with her sweet mug of sarcasm.

"I guess, it's better I start getting used to it," I tell myself

"Right !! … Reaction causes more reactions!" a thought pops up.

"Hey Poo, how come you are early today … AL told me, that you would be coming late today," Mehul interrupts my thoughts.

"Hmm … actually, the plan got cancelled," Pooja responds

"Okay … I guess we should start … and to start off, I have some good news for you guys," I say

"You proposed to HJ and she said Yes?" Pooja asks (typical girl)

"Give me a break!!" Mehul blurts out, "Are you crazy … This ass has not yet told his feelings to Rochelle … And he has known and loved her since school days… Proposing HJ … IMPOSSIBLE!"

"What?? … Alban you like Rochelle!!!" Pooja is taken by surprise. I tell you, these girls hear only the gossipy part of the stories. "Now I need not tell Rochelle about it … Grapevine will do my job," I tell myself (Phew).

"Thank you Mehul," I say and ask, "Shall I continue with my good news?"

"Hmm … Yes please," Mehul tries to imitate Mr. Tendel.

"I have understood what a bottleneck is … Thanks to Pooja" I proclaim

"What … Really … What is it??" Mehul asks

"Me … how … when" confused Pooja joins in.

I did not want to give them the answer directly, so I went to the board and write—

Goal: HJ and I have to reach college

We both meet at Dadar railway station and then proceed to college.

Time taken to reach from office to Dadar

AL - **25 mins**

HJ - **35 mins**

Time taken to reach from Dadar to college - **15 mins.**

I turn and ask, "so what is the time taken to complete the process?"

"Complete the process??" Pooja looks confused and asks, "I didn't get you"

"Assume the process ends with both of us reaching college," I say, "Even if one of us reaches college, the process is still incomplete."

"Simple!" Mehul says, "you take 25+15 that is 40 minutes, and she takes 35+15 that is 50 minutes ... so the whole process is going to take at least 50 minutes"

"Hmm ... that is correct," I say, "But I can reach in 40 minutes"

"What are you trying to prove?" Pooja asks in a confused tone.

"See, we both are resources right? ... No matter how less time I take to reach, my performance is limited by HJ ... isn't it?"

"Got it … You could have reached in 40 minutes, if HJ had reached Dadar in 25 minutes… So HJ is the bottleneck," Mehul rejoices

"Hmm … Correct … I noticed that while travelling too," Pooja says

"How?" I ask

"When the roads are empty, it takes 8 minutes to reach office from my home," she says "and in traffic conditions it takes 25 minutes"

"Traffic is the bottleneck," Mehul says

"Cool, so I guess we all are on same page as far as understanding the bottleneck," I say, "Now the second biggest question is …"

"What would be our systems bottleneck?" Pooja helps me complete my statement.

"I think I got a clue," Mehul says and picks up the marker and goes towards the board and writes

Capacity table

Max number of Documents presented by customer - **100 docs**

Max number of Documents which can be scanned for processing - **500 docs**

Max number of Document we can process - **128 docs** (as per Tendel's email)

"From the look of it…" Mehul says in a confused tone "the bottleneck in our case is the customer"

There is silence now. I stare at those numbers on the board and start wondering whether our understanding is wrong again. That's when the lighting struck me, "Hold on, there is something wrong there."

"Yes … You are right … if that was the case, we would not have so much of backlog" Pooja says before I could complete my point.

"Mehul can you please replicate the capacity table," I say, "But don't include the last processing part" He does as I say and it looks like this now

Capacity table

Max number of Documents presented by customer - **100 docs**

Max number of Documents which can be scanned for processing - **500 docs**

I take the marker from Mehul and tell them "There are two sub processes in the next step that is, data input of Document processing, and Authorization (checking) of documents, which is done by two different resources … Right??"

They nod in agreement as this is the Model (maker-checker) followed by us.

"And there are two different groups of people doing this... Right?" I emphasize

"Yes the senior experienced staff authorize the transactions, whereas the relatively new guys key in the data (data input) for the transactions," Mehul replies.

"So, how many makers (one who does data input) do we have?" I ask

"Ten," Mehul responds.

"And what is their capacity?" I ask

"15 docs on an average in a day," Mehul says

"So capacity of makers is 150 docs (10 x 15) ... Right?" I say that and write it on the board.

Capacity table

Max number of Documents presented by customer –
100 docs

Max number of Documents which can be scanned for processing – **500 docs**

Max number of Document data inputted by makers –
150 docs (10 x 15)

"And how many checkers do we have??" I ask.

"Six," Mehul replies

"Okay... So the checker's capacity is ..." before I could complete Mehul says "12 documents ... which means the authorizing capacity is 12 docs x 5 checkers = 60 documents"

"From where did you get five... earlier you mentioned there are six checkers" Pooja counters his calculations

"Hmm ... yes ... Six includes Ajit, and he is always busy on the phone with his girl... So I excluded him," Mehul replies and we all laugh nodding our heads. However, I write on the actuals on the board and it looks like this

Capacity table

Max number of Documents presented by the customer – **100 docs**

Max number of Documents which can be scanned for processing – **500 docs**

Max number of Document data inputted by the makers – **150 docs (10 x 15)**

Max number of Document authorized by the checkers – **72 docs (6 x 12)**

The whole picture is clear now. Without any doubts, the checkers i.e. the senior and experienced staff are the bottlenecks.

"It's surprising that we … The Checkers are the bottlenecks!!" Mehul comments.

"They limit the performance of the whole system," Pooja comments

"How ironic…" I say, "and they expect seniors to manage the process and do less of processing."

"Numbers we have arrived on, is based on the assumption that, Ajit does 15 docs whereas he hardly authorizes a single doc," Mehul says, "and also assuming that there is no absenteeism"

"Mehul is right," Pooja says, "so the realistic capacity is less than 60 documents i.e. the capacity of the system is capacity for the authorizers/ checkers (the bottleneck)"

"That is a startling realization," I say "100 docs given by customers and we could manage only 60. No wonder why the documents were piling up day by day"

"So what's next?" Pooja asks

"The next thing is … I need to give back a fitting reply to Mr. Tendel, that his calculation is wrong," I say.

"Yes, you are right… we need to give him back … and that too strongly" Mehul encourages me. However, Pooja does not seem to be impressed by the idea, so I ask her "what is the matter with you?? What are you thinking?"

"Hmm … I was just wondering…" she says expecting me to poke further

"What …what are you wondering," I oblige.

"Whether giving back Mr. Tendel would help us make more money??" she says, "Are we increasing our throughput… by any chance??"

Her question dissolves our enthusiasm and our heads go down.

"Nopes…" Mehul says like an innocent kid.

"So, why are we doing it? … Let us focus our attention on things, which will help us increase our throughput" Pooja rightly stresses.

"You are right Pooja," I say, "Guess… I got carried away."

"Okay … So what's next??" Pooja asks.

"We need to call Prof. Irani," Mehul says.

I dial the number and the phone rings "Hey …Irani here," this time I hear a fresh voice

"Good Morning…sir," I say.

"Good Evening AL… Not Morning," he replies, "I expected you to call"

"Good evening sir…" I correct myself.

"Okay so you have identified the bottleneck," he asks.

"Yes sir and they are the authorizers," I say.

"Senior guys right?" he says, "by the way, how did you arrive at this conclusion??"

"Why is he asking the process of identifying bottleneck when he knows the bottleneck is right," I tell myself.

"He has not yet said that it is correct," a thought pops up.

"Hello … hello… AL… are you there??"

"Yeah sir … I was going through the notes," I lie.

"Stop fooling me AL … I know what you are thinking … Why does this guy wants to know the process, when the bottleneck is correct... Right?" Prof Irani correctly guesses.

"How the hell did he come to know this?? Was I loud when I spoke to myself??" I ask myself.

"Al stop thinking and tell me fast … I have a meeting to attend in the next five minutes," Prof Irani says, "It is important for me know the process you followed."

"We divided our process into sub processes… at a very high level," I say, "customers submitting docs, scanning process, creating (making) process, authorizing (checking) process"

"Hmm … Go ahead," he says.

"Then we determined max capacity of each process," I say

"Can you provide me the numbers," he says and I read out to him the capacity table.

"Customer capacity - 100 docs, Scanning capacity - 500 docs, Makers capacity - 10 makers doing 15 docs in a day that is 150 docs and Checkers capacity - 6 checkers authorizing 12 docs in a day that is 72 docs."

"So the authorizers/checkers are the bottleneck," he says

"Yes … Although the figures show 72 … It is the maximum capacity … However in reality it is around 60," I say

"How??" Prof Irani asks

"Ajit my manager does not process a single transaction and absenteeism," I say, "However while calculating the capacity, I have included them"

"Never mind," He says, "you are right in identifying the bottleneck. Now you see why there are so many rollovers."

"Yes sir …We have understood the importance i.e. the throughput of the system is defined by them … the bottlenecks" I respond

"Rightly said," he says

"So now, what's next sir?" I ask.

"What you did was the first step of the five focusing steps," he says

"Five??" I say

"Yes, five … Now take down the next two steps," he says, "and these two steps would start making a difference."

"Start making a difference??" I repeat

"Yes … It would … whatever you have done so far, has just started the engine," he says, "these steps will help you turn the car wheels in motion"

"Great…" I say in desperation. Pooja and Mehul are smiling and reacting as if they can hear what the prof is speaking.

"Note down the steps," he says

"Exploit the bottleneck to its maximum," he says, "a single minute wasted by your authorizers would reduce the system's capacity. And once lost, you can't get it back"

"Okay," I say and note down—exploit the systems bottlenecks

"Share their load with the resources that have excess capacity where ever possible" I note this down also.

"Seems logical … isn't it?" Prof. Irani says

"Yeah … and simple too," I say

"Right …they are simple," he says, "you know, what the problem is with humans … They assume, if the problem is complex, the solution should be even more complex."

Even I was assuming the same thing, I wonder☹

"The solutions are simple, you just have to find the root cause and simple solutions would emerge," he enlightens us

"Hmm … Okay sir," I say (I don't think I have an option to say anything else)

"Okay then … All the very best," he says, "your next call to me should have details of the improvements"

"Bye sir"

"Bye … And give your girl my regards" he says and hangs up, and I wonder which girl he was referring to.

CHAPTER 11

Utilizing the bottleneck to the fullest

I write down the three points as suggested by Professor Irani

- ✓ Exploit the Bottleneck
- ✓ Subordinate the tasks done by Bottlenecks to non-bottlenecks
- ✓ Time lost by the bottlenecks means systems capacity reduced.

I give them time to read and digest the statements. "Hmm … I don't understand," Mehul says as he scratches his head

"Same here … I am lost too," Pooja says

"What are the Bottlenecks??" I ask them

"Authorizers" Pooja replies

"So we need to exploit them fully," I say, "Authorizers should be used fully."

"HOW??" Mehul is offended, "AREN'T WE ALREADY FULLY EXPLOITED"

"How, I don't know, but they should not be under utilized for sure," I aggravate him further

"Non bottlenecks … that is the makers (inputters) will share their load," Pooja says, "Is it correct for point two?"

"Yeah … Precisely!!" I say. By now I am convinced that the suggestions provided by Professor would work.

"Last point is confusing," Mehul is still scratching his head. That makes me wonder that he is not scratching his head over this problem, rather it is his ugly dandruff, which is falling all over ☺

"What is the system's capacity?" I ask

"It is…" Pooja replies, but I interrupt her by saying, "Let Mehul answer". He looks at the board and then says "72 documents"

"Isn't that the capacity of the bottlenecks too?" I ask him

"Hmm…" Mehul nods

"So if you and me waste time being an authorizer, what will happen?" I ask.

"Your performance will go down," he says.

"Which means, I would authorize fewer docs… won't I?" I say, "that is the number of docs processed would be less… Correct?"

Both of them are humming and nodding.

"Which in turn will reduce our throughput," I conclude.

"I can construe something from the three statements," Pooja says

"What is it??" I ask

"All three suggestions, strive to enhance the capacity of the Bottlenecks (Authorizers)," Pooja concludes.

"Wow, it's so true" I wonder, "So I guess, we should focus on finding ways to increase the capacity of the bottlenecks."

"How do we do it is a million dollar question," Mehul asks

A brilliant idea struck me "Why don't we brainstorm?"

"What is brainstorm??" Mehul asks

"This is something I learnt in college," I say and continue, "Brainstorming is a technique by which efforts are made to find a conclusion for a particular problem by gathering a list of ideas spontaneously contributed by its members."

"Not a bad idea … Let us brainstorm then," Pooja says.

"By we, I meant the whole team," I say, "more heads, the better it is when we brainstorm"

"Sounds perfect … More the merrier!!" Mehul seconds

"I guess, we should take a break for now … But let our minds still work on this," I say, "come up with ideas to increase the capacity of authorizers"

Next day the whole team is in the meeting room, and I wonder how come the whole team is present. Usually, for such meetings people are reluctant to join. Going by experience hardly 50% of them join and the fact that it is scheduled after working hours, the percentage drops even further. I am sure Mehul might have cooked up some story, that's why they all are here. I call Mehul and ask him slowly "how come the whole team is present here."

"Hehe … I told them there is some very important news … and you are going to share it with them now," Mehul whispers.

"Great … Now I have to cook something up," I tell myself.

"Tell the truth," a thought pops up.

"Hello everybody," I say

"Hey... hi... hello... Yeah," is what I hear when they respond.

"Okay ... to start just an update on what's happening," I say, "we are not making money, the throughput is not enough to sustain"

They all have a blank look on their face and right at the end Pooja and Mehul are giggling.

"Okay ... Sorry guys ... for being so technical," I say

"I guess ... MBA has gone into your head," Ray sarcastically says, and they all start giggling now.

"Whatever!!" I ignore his comment and continue, "The point is we are not delivering as per the customer's expectations. Branches aren't happy, and Singapore Branch has threatened to take away the process if there are no significant improvements."

The giggling is stopped by now.

"Are we going to lose our jobs?" Reshma innocently asks

"I don't know dear," I empathize and try to give them some hope, "But if we improve significantly we would not only stay, but enjoy healthy bonuses"

"So you have called us here to give a 'pep talk' or what!!" Ray starts throwing his usual tantrums.

"Nopes ... I need your help. I need your help to turn the fortunes around," I say, rather beg.

"We are with you," Reshma says.

Taking them through the whole process would be time consuming, I wonder.

"So how will these people realize the importance of what you are gonna ask them" I ask myself. A brilliant story struck me then

"We are here to Brainstorm," I say and everybody is still having the poker face, so I continue "But before I tell you what to brainstorm on, I would like to share a short story"

The word 'story' brings on some changes in their facial expressions. They all are attentive, including Ray, and they nod their heads.

"I guess they have no choice... Hehe," I tell myself.

"The story goes like this," I say—

"There was a shipping company which recently bought a second hand vessel for their operations. However after few days of operation it stalled. Attempts by the best engineers failed to get the vessel moving. Then some suggested about an old man who repairs barges. The management was not very keen on it, as brilliant engineers who tried to fix the problem were unsuccessful, what this barge mechanic would do. As there was no harm in giving him a shot, they let him too. The old man inspected the ship in and out for four hours and then finally stopped at a spot. He removed a small hammer from his tool kit and gently tapped a few time on the machine. He then asked the captain to check if the ship is working. To everybody's surprise the ship indeed started. The CEO of the company was very pleased and asked him to come over for tea. 'So what are your charges' the CEO asked, '5 lakhs rupees' was his reply. '5 lakh for tapping on the machine' the surprised CEO asked. 'Nopes ... That cost only 10,' he said, 'Rs. 4,99,990 for knowing where to hit'☺"

I wait for some time so that they understand and digest the story.

Mehul comes close to me and slowly asks, "What's the whole point dude??"

I smile and continue, "so friends like the old man we have identified the spot and we need your help to tap it too"

"What's that spot??" Ray asks. It seems he got involved in the story.

"Okay, the spot is the 'authorizers' in our process. We need to increase their capacity to start our ship," I say, "So here we are to brainstorm on ideas, that will increase the capacity of the authorizers." There is a silence… pin drop silence.

"You guys with me??" I try to motivate "are we going to FIGHT or FLIGHT??"

"FIGHT!!!" Ray shouts and everybody join in his shout. I was happy too, as it is always good to have people like Ray on your side.

"Ok then let's start," I say, "But before we begin… Am not sure how many of you are aware of the rules for a Brainstorming activity …Nevertheless …Mehul please explain to them the rules"

Mehul starts explaining, **"Rule 1**—Let the ideas flow in, don't hesitate ... Just give your ideas ... No matter how small, big, funny, serious, etc. Whatever are the ideas, just speak out.

Rule 2—At this stage all ideas are to be treated equally

Rule 3 and the most significant one—No idea should be criticized. No one should pass judgment on any idea.

Rule 4—One can build up on somebody else's idea"

"I didn't get the fourth rule," Ray interrupts.

I could feel the lava inside Mehul now. He just can't stand Ray talk. Before the lava could erupt, I interrupt, "For example, Mehul gives an idea that eggs are good for authorizer's health and thus increases performance". Now Reshma adds on to it, "On a long run to reduce costs we should buy hens that can lay eggs for us." Everyone laughs on my silly example.

"No idea is small," Mehul reminds them in a funny voice

'I think we would also need COCKS," Pooja says trying to build up the idea.

"Thanks Pooja," I say in a sarcastic tone, "Can we move on Mehul … or else instead of data processing we would be raising our own poultry"

"**Rule 5**—The person with most ideas would get a pizza treat from Alban" Mehul declares

This rule startles me. "What!! … Where did this come from," I shouted at Mehul in my mind. He smiled at me and winked, as if he heard what I said in my mind.

"Okay, let's start," Mehul says as he comes and stands next to me.

"What the heck was the fifth rule?" I asked

"I just felt like eating pizza ... so added this rule," he said with a cunning smile on his face

"And what makes you think, that you'll win?" I ask

"I would … Just wait and watch," he replied.

There is silence in the room, and I guess everyone is waiting for the other to start. Maybe this was the first time for most of them in the team, to speak out, that is why this silence, I wonder.

"Come on guys… don't tell me we are unable to generate a single idea to increase productivity of the authorizers" I try to motivate. Generally, people are proactive in advising others how to improve, but today why is no one is speaking up, I wonder.

"Maybe they are scared about the situation (Lay off)," I tell myself

"No chance!! … You are a useless leader, who simply cannot motivate his team" a de-motivating thought pops up☹.

"Maybe they need a kick start," another idea pops up. Yes, they need a start, and hence I gesture Mehul to start.

"I have an IDEA!" Mehul obliges.

"Liar… You use Vodafone … don't you??" Ray cracks a silly joke and the room bursts into laughter. Mehul dint like it a bit and I could see that from his artificial smile.

"Good joke Ray..." I intervene, "However let's get into serious business now ... Mehul please continue"

"Okay ... My idea is ... since authorizer's potential for scrutiny is 60 documents in practical terms, and we receive 90 to 100 documents every day, then I believe we should hire more authorizers," Mehul says.

"Not possible..." Ray comments and before he could continue Mehul interrupts him and says, "Rule three my friend... you cannot pass a judgment." He was right, in a brainstorming exercise one should not do that, but before I could voice out my agreement, Ray counters, "There is a universal rule for any meeting, let the person talking complete, and then you can comment. Moreover, please refer your rule 4"

Everyone including me looks at the board where the rules were written.

"It says one can build upon others idea," Ray says, "so let me finish."

"I am sorry ... Go ahead," Mehul responds with a forceful artificial apology.

"Not possible ... as I don't think, in this recessionary period if anyone would want to hire new staff and that too an experienced & costly one. However,

Mehul idea is partially good… That is, instead of hiring from outside let us promote a senior maker to a checker (Authorizer)" Ray builds a case for his promotion☺.

"That makes sense," I tell myself.

"Okay, that makes sense, increase capacity… externally or internally," I say, "now let's focus more on increasing the productivity of the authorizers, I mean the existing ones"

"Productivity can be increased if the authorizers do productive work" Ray comments

"What do you mean to say … we don't work?" Mehul takes that personally.

"I didn't say that," Ray says in a very soft tone.

"Ok… So what are you coming to?" I ask Ray trying to understand why there is this perception on floor that managers and authorizers don't do much productive work.

"See, you all say, you guys are monitoring the workflow queues, priority, makers if they are productive, etc." Ray says.

"Yeah… But that is required, otherwise your(makers) productivity will go down" Mehul defends.

"Yeah, but if you keep doing that then who will authorize the transactions?" Ray comments

"I think… he has a point" I say "Makers are non bottlenecks and their productivity won't impact the throughput, unless they themselves become bottlenecks"

"How??" Mehul questions

"See we as authorizers have only 10 hours in a day… Right?" I ask.

"So if we work like machines we can authorize 20 docs… Considering half an hour per document… Right?" I ask, and he nods his head.

"So every minute we do something else apart from authorizing we are losing out capacity and in a way becoming less productive," I say

"Exactly…that's what I meant," Ray intervenes.

"So you mean to say all of us should just do authorizing??" Mehul counter question me

"And besides, it is an important task…We just can't ignore it," Pooja supports Mehul

"So what should be done?" I ask the group.

"I think all six authorizers should not do this monitoring stuff... maybe one or two should do it" Daphane (one of the quietest girls in the team) says.

"Good … that makes sense too," I tell myself.

"But then, handling customer queries would be one of those things which the authorizers do apart from authorizing," I say.

"Yeah... Like going to the loo," Mehul comments at a lighter note.

"Yes you right in that too..." I say, "but the whole point is that, we need to identify this list ... A list of non value add"

"The one, which I had made for the process?" Mehul asks

"Yeah ... But the one you did was on the whole process, we should focus our value analysis on the bottlenecks only ... that is authorizers," I say

"What is value analysis?" Daphane asks.

I see the same question on some other faces. so I define it for them, "It is an exercise whereby we distinguish activities done for a process into value adding and non value adding"

"And how do you define value adding?" Ray asks

"I mean something which is of value for you, might not be for me"

"That is right," I reply, "Hence the value should be aligned to the goal or objective for which those activities are carried on"

"So you mean to say, in our case all the activities which help authorizing a transaction would be value add and those which is not related or required for authorizing would be non value add" Ray tries to confirm his understanding.

"Precisely!" I say, "Answering customer query is one example of non value adding activity... in that sense"

"But then it is an important and required activity," Mehul says in a defending tone

"Yeah ... But it is still a non-value add activity with respect to the goal" Ray says in a firm tone.

"But an important one!!" Mehul repeats himself in a more firm and loud tone. Before it gets out of control, I intervene and say, "Guys ... Relax... You both are right"

"How??" Mehul asks wondering how he and Ray are correct.

"Let's change the approach of distinguishing an activity," I say and go to the board. I draw a quadrant, which looks like this

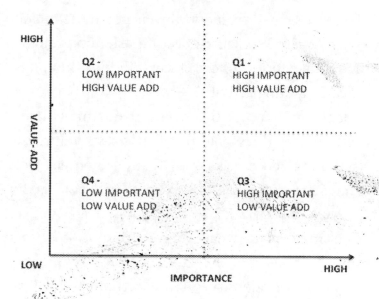

They all look at me with a blank face.

"Let us classify the activities done by the authorizers based on two aspects," I say and point towards the board.

"Value-add or not," I say and take a pause for them to digest and continue, "and whether they are Important or not"

"I did not get you?" Mehul asks

"Ok… Let me explain … say for example … Queries," I say, "What kind of activity is this? Is it Important?"

"Yes it is," Mehul says.

"Now tell me is it value adding as per the definition we discussed sometime back," I ask him again

He thinks for a while and says, "I don't think it is a value adding activity"

"Bazinga!" I say, "So this would go quadrant three"

"But what's the whole point in classifying these activities." Pooja asks, and I can see on her face that she was finding this exercise of classification a 'NON-VALUE ADD'.

"Let me explain what we are going to do" I say and she nods

"Step 1—we identify all the activities which a bottleneck (authorizer) does

Step 2—we place them in the respective quadrant based on the value they are adding and its importance."

They all look at me and especially Pooja, she gives me a cold stare, which meant 'CRAP'

"You have still not answered my question," Pooja says in a frustrated tone.

"Just chill Pooja… Let me explain the importance of quadrants" I say and scribble on the diagram I made earlier and explain them.

"**Quadrant one**—Important and value adding … here authorizers have to do these activities and can't ignore them.

Quadrant two—Value adding but not important...
these activities where ever possible should be
delegated to the makers

Quadrant three—Non value add but important...
Even this should be treated like Quadrant two

Quadrant four—Non value add and Not
important ... Ideally these activities should not be
done at all." I conclude and wait for their reaction.

"Now that makes sense..." Pooja is visibly relieved.

"How does it make sense???" Ray asks. I know
where he was coming from and I say, "Let me
explain... Ray," He gestures me to continue

"Thank you," I say sarcastically and continue,
"See, we have excess capacity for makers whereas
authorizers are short in capacity... You agree?"

"Yeah ... that is a fact," he says

"So makers have some excess time in hand?" I
rephrase the previous question to emphasize my
point.

"Hmm...yeah you can say that," Ray nods

"So if we share some work which the authorizers
do, with the makers, it should not affect the makers
existing output?" I ask again, and he thinks for a
while and then nods.

"However, these activities which were done by the
authorizers are not there anymore, and they can

focus on quadrant one activities i.e. authorizing transaction and thereby increasing their output... Right?" I ask him again. This time he thinks for a while and then says, "yeah ... It would probably" "And as you know, authorizer's output is the teams output, since they are the bottlenecks ... so the whole teams output will increase, right?" I tell him and take a deep breath.

"Hmm ... Yes, it makes sense," he says and finally, I felt mission accomplished.

For the next half an hour, we list down activities, and classify them in the appropriate quadrants. I look at the diagram and wonder, thank God, I attended the 'Time management' training class.

"It was the Urgent/Important matrix which you copied, amended and applied here, wasn't it?" a thought pops, and I smile.

"That's enough for now ... I guess," Pooja comments and I look at her (I am still smiling)

"Something funny!!" she asks.

"Oh ...nothing ... I was wondering something," I say, "Anyway ... I guess we have made a pretty good progress and it was a very productive discussion. I will let you know the changes in the process flow. Hopefully, that should make a difference."

"A POSITIVE difference," Pooja quickly corrects me.

"Ok then … Thanks a lot, for your time, see you tomorrow," I say and we all disperse. Meanwhile, Mehul comes to me and asks, "What time are we meeting tomorrow?"

"As usual 8 am, we need to implement these process changes by tomorrow itself." I say.

"Hey Alban…" Ray interrupts, "Can I join you guys?"

"Yeah sure... Why not!" I instinctively reply.

"Oouchh!!" a thought popped up.

"What happened?" I ask myself.

"Look… Mehul is throwing stares at you" I talk to myself

And I look at Mehul (who is still frowning and staring for allowing Ray) and I say, "Oouch!!"

We all come out of the meeting room and the entire floor is empty except one workstation.

"Hey why is Rochelle sitting so late?" Mehul asks and briskly walks towards her desk... (Obviously, to flirt.)

"Hey Rochelle," Mehul says "what happened ?? Why are you sitting so late??"

"Dog … Never leaves a chance to flirt," I wonder and since the floor was all empty, I could hear everything they were talking. But I guess they were not aware of this.

"Oh nothing, had some work," Rochelle replies.

"Some work, she is not the one who sits late," I wonder again.

"When are you leaving? Should I drop you?" Mr. flirty makes his first move.

"Dog!!" I murmur.

"Hmm … No thanks … You carry on, I still have some tasks to complete," she replies.

"Hehe… yes yes" I laugh in my thoughts and punch in the air ☺.

"Ok … I'll wait," Mehul says. I see Rochelle is now getting a bit restless, and she says.

"Actually Mehul … I was waiting for Alban," she confesses.

"Alban … That's me … She is waiting for me …. WUPPPEEE," I get delighted

"Oh … Okay," Mehul says in disappointment.

"Can you please pass on the message to him," she says and Mehul obliges. I go to her desk and ask,

"So… Somebody is waiting for me today… where did the sun rise from today?"

"Hmm…" she smiles

"How come? Is everything ok?" I try to break the ice.

"Until now everything was ok ... But..." she stops speaking

"But what?" I ask her wondering whether everything is fine at her home

"But it's getting too late, you'll drop me home na??" she asks and just then my mobile beeps. Its HJ's text message and it reads "hey AL baby ... wru nt 2 b seen in collge, missin u :-* ... poss to meet tonite ... For an actual coffee"

"What happened?? You are coming na??" Rochelle asks me again.

"Of course I am, ..." I say and simultaneously I sms HJ that I would meet her after the lecture. I don't know why I did that, maybe I didn't want either of them to feel sad by my rejection or maybe I didn't want to disappoint anybody (including me). It was a very tight schedule... But I enjoyed the company of both and I guess even they had a good time too. On my way back, I was wondering whether having multiple choices is really a good thing? I mean in situations where one can select one option when all are equally good? Lots of questions were running through my mind and I thought to pen them down and take my team's opinion on it tomorrow. I wrote the below—

I am confused, lot of questions running through my mind, and I am quite anxious to know the answer to these questions. But the question that is bothering me the most is ... whether it is better to be in a position wherein you have choices to make or a situation wherein you are left with no choice, but to eat what's there on your plate? You might think on the first cut; it's always better to have choices, and no prizes for guessing that even I used to think the same, until I started reflecting on it. Let me explain... Let's ignore the 'having choices' part and take the disregarded one i.e. 'eat what's there on your plate'. Let me begin with an example of physical appearance (except for hogging obesity!!). So the question here is... are you happy with your physical appearance? (We don't have a choice here) I am sure most of us are not. There would be something or the other, which you won't like, maybe it's your ear, nose, your eyes, etc. And if you think otherwise, then maybe you have accepted it as a fact...by heart and you are happy now. Let me take another example, I travel every day between Virar and Churchgate (60kms), got no options here (at least for now :-)). I have accepted this fact by heart, and this problem does not bother me anymore. In fact, I have taken it as a cradle for me and I try to catch up on sleep while travelling. So now

I am happy about this. Net net ... what I can conclude is, Once you accept the fact by heart (I mean ... you have stopped cribbing about it) for which you have no choice, you will start finding happiness in them. They would become a platform for your dreams. And dreams are our subconscious efforts towards goal setting. I need not explain further how important goals are in our lives. So to conclude, I can say nine out of ten times in a long run, having no choice is not as bad as we might think it is. In fact, it's good to have no choice at times. The reason, I said 'its good' not 'its better', because it would be unfair if I don't take into consideration the state of having choices. So this brings us to a general notion, that is, whether having choices is always better?

Decision-making is a product of choices. What I mean is, if there are no choices ... Decision making would not exist. Decision-making is the most important part of our lives and across the globe. Have you ever wondered why management personnel are paid so high? One of the most important reasons for that is their ability to take decisions. No wonder why management institutes are minting money. It's because people go there to learn this art, the art of decision-making. So if you have choices, then we need a very good, intuitive ability to make perfect decisions. And it's a known fact that no one is 100 % perfect in making decisions or for that matter, anything. And if the decision goes well ... We might say its better to have choices, and if it doesn't ... It leaves a sore mark, which is more difficult to accept than accepting something that we have no choice for. I did not have a choice today to sleep in the train as I did not get a place to sit. So I thought of writing this, and now that I am about to reach Virar my destination, I leave this topic for you guys to conclude... I'm still confused!!"

"Wow!!! I wrote an article." I tell myself and feel proud about it. However, back of my mind, I am convinced that having no choices is better. "Look at the situation you are in now." I say to myself.

"Which situation?" thought pops. "Is it 'HJ or Rochelle' crisis or is it 'office' crisis?"

"Office crisis ... Obviously!!!" I shout. A guy passing by, stares at me and wonders if I have gone mad.

"Relax dude ..." thought pops up again and I calmly walk back home.

CHAPTER 12

Everything else is second priority

Next day, I make Mehul and Pooja read my article and ask them for their opinion on whether it is good to have choice or not. "What the hell is this?" Mehul says "I mean ... I am getting cramps in my head."

"C'mon Mehul ... It not that bad," Pooja says, "You have written it well Al."

"Okay Okay ... what's the whole point you are trying to make here?" Mehul asks.

"Nothing ... just wanted to understand if having choices is better or not having them," I say.

"So what do you feel?" Mehul asks me.

"I feel, having no choices is better." I say.

"Rubbish … I feel having choices is always better," Mehul counters.

"I think Al is right, and I agree with him," Pooja as usual counters Mehul.

"Yeah, that's pretty obvious that you would agree to Al," Mehul passes a judgment☺.

"What's so obvious?" Pooja asks him.

"You will always take the other person's side when I am on one side," Mehul finally blurts out what he felt.

"No… that's not the case, given a particular situation …" she says and starts wondering

"Go ahead …" Mehul says.

"See … in a particular situation, whether you have a choice or not, again, is not in your hand. You have no choice in the first place, isn't it?" she says.

"Hmm …" Mehul wonders for a while and says, "makes sense."

"So… I guess we are in a better situation," I say.

"Better situation … How??" Pooja sounds confused.

"Yeah, better off … I mean the situation we are in now is not by choice," I say and all of us laugh.

"Ok, let's get back to business," Pooja says.

"Hmm … I guess we are done with our warm up discussion, and we can start," I say.

"So, from where do we start now?" Mehul asks.

"Let us quickly identify the non-value adding activities done by the authorizers, which we can either remove or delegate." I say, meanwhile Pooja gets up and walks towards the white board, and it seems like she is searching something. Maybe a marker, I guess, but still I ask her.

"What are you searching for Pooja?"

"Don't tell me you looking out for non-value adding activities there... Hehe," Mehul cracks a silly sarcastic joke.

"Nopes ... Searching for your 25 paisa (25% of a brain) here," She says.

"Okay guys... don't start again," I say, "By the way, what exactly are you trying to do Poo?"

"I've already identified few non value adding activities and was trying to list it down on the board," she says.

"Ohh..." Mehul says and slowly slides the marker towards Pooja, and pretends as if no one saw. Pooja gives him a Dracula stare, and starts writing the non-value adding activities. Below is what she has written.

Following are the activities without which authorization process can happen (non value add)
1. Compliance checks

2. Queries
3. Monitoring workflow
4. Monitoring team members
5. Reports preparation for management
6. Meetings

"This is all I could think of," Pooja says, "but you can add few more to this … If any."

"How can you say that monitoring team members and handling queries are non-value add activities?" As usual, Mehul gets very defensive, "Its part of the process."

Mehul has a point here, I wonder but the same is washed away when Pooja replies

"Precisely … They are part of the whole process, but as per the definition of value, they are in congruence to our goal… isn't it?" She asks.

"I didn't get you… congo what?" Mehul counters.

"Ok … Answer this," Pooja says, "In a day how many queries do you handle approximately?"

"Hmm … Around 10 to 15," he says.

"So, suppose you handle 50 queries one day," Pooja says and takes a pause to look at me

"Yeah, go ahead…" I say in curiosity.

"So what would be the result?" she asks, "I mean how many more documents would you authorize…

this is related to our objective… i.e. exploiting the bottleneck"

"Are you nuts!!" he says "How can I authorize more, in fact, it would be the other way round… I mean, I would authorize lesser documents"

"She is smart!!" I tell myself.

"That's my point Mehul… The more you handle queries, the lesser you will authorize transactions," Pooja replies.

"Hmm … Got it," Mehul replies, "It's important but non-value adding, and it reduces my capacity to authorize transactions. Thereby, it reduces the processing capacity, which further limits the output. Less out means less revenue, and less revenue means less/no money we receive… That means we are not achieving our goal."

"Mehul … Well summarized!!" I say.

"So then in that case, delegation/assignment of work is also a non value add" Mehul concludes.

"Hmm… That makes sense." Pooja says and writes it down on the board.

"Guys…" I say, "I think we have missed something very important here."

"What's that??" Mehul asks.

"We have covered almost everything." Pooja says.

"REWORK !!" I say.

"Oh yeah…" Pooja says, "It's the most useless, non-value adding activity."

"Yes, you are right," I say, "I believe we could save a lot of time if we reduce the rework."

"So here is the final list of non-value add activities." I say and we all stare at the board

1. Rework
2. Compliance checks
3. Queries
4. Monitoring workflow
5. Monitoring team members
6. Reports preparation for management
7. Meetings
8. Assigning work-items to the makers

There is a long silence, as we stare at the list on the board.

"So what's next?" Mehul breaks the silence.

"Cause-effect analysis," I say.

"What's that analysis?" Pooja enquires.

"I remember professor Irani's words," I say, "Most of the time, the problems are symptoms and not the disease itself"

"Sorry … Didn't understand," Mehul is confused.

"Say for example, you have a high temperature," I try to give a analogy "High temperature is a symptom, whereas viral fever might me the disease"

"Hmm ... but I still did not get your analogy" Mehul confesses

"What I mean is, the items in the list are all effects and not causes," I say, "What we need to do is to identify the root cause of the listed effects. We should ask ourselves WHY is this effect happening? What are the causes?"

"Ohh ... So once you identify the cause we should address it," Pooja tries to confirm her understanding.

"Got it, so you mean to say we identify the disease and then cure it" Mehul adds.

"Precisely... And one more interesting fact!!" I say, "You get to a root cause by asking FIVE WHYs"

"FIVE WHY's?" Now Pooja is confused.

"By repeatedly asking the question 'why?' (use five as a rule of thumb), you can peel away the layers of an issue, just like the layers of an onion, which can lead you to the root cause of the problem. The reason for the problem can often lead to another question. You may need to ask the question fewer or more than five times before you get to the origin of the problem," I explain

"Got it ... So from which effect do you guys want to start and try this?" Pooja says excitedly

"Hmm ... Let's take queries," Mehul says.

"Ok..." I say and make two columns and mention 'I' and 'Others' as the header.

"What are these two column for?" Mehul asks.

"Have patience... you'll come to know soon," I say, "So tell me WHY(1st) do we have to handle queries?" I ask.

"Hmm ... because branches or customer have some queries and its part of our job to address their queries," Mehul says.

"WHY (2nd) do branches or say customers have queries?" I ask again.

"Majority of cases are because the customers or branches are not able to understand our observations," Pooja says.

"And others?" I ask.

"Others are due to lack of their knowledge on this product," She says.

"For the second point (others) I guess we can't do much..." I say, "at the most we can suggest that training is required for customers and branch users (sending locations)."

And I write "TRAINING REQUIRED FOR BRANCHES/CUSTOMER" in the 'Others' column. I can see on their faces those question marks on why this bifurcation i.e. OTHERS and I. Nevertheless I continue, "Going to the first part, why don't they understand our observations?" I ask.

There is a silence for a while, and I break it by answering, "Our observations are not user friendly." They both ponder over my point.

"But then, if we give them an easy to understand, detailed observation ... Won't that be spoon feeding?" Mehul asks.

"I agree, they are paid for their jobs too ... they ought to be a little smart," Pooja seconds Mehul

"Will this spoon feeding help us achieve our goal?" I ask, and Mehul thinks for a while and hesitantly answers "Yes it will... I guess"

"So why not do it!" I say and mention 'USER FRIENDLY OBSERVATIONS' in 'I' column.

"So what's next?" I ask.

"Compliance checks !!" Mehul says, "I hate them."

"Hmm ... Compliance checks..." I say, "why do we (authorizers) have to do it... and not they (makers/inputters)"

"I don't know ... that's the way it has been for so many years." Mehul says.

"This reminds me a story of a Sadhu and his pet cat," I say.

"Story time," Pooja brightens up and I begin

Once upon a time, there lived a sadhu and had a pet cat, which he loved, as though it were his own child. The little cat followed his master wherever he went. While the Sadhu was performing the 'puja' and recited his prayers, the cat would move freely all over the place, upsetting the sacred utensils and disturbing its master and his devotees.

To prevent such disturbance and profanation the Sadhu, before starting his puja, began tying the cat to the big banyan tree. With the passing of time, this became a standard practice. Once the cat was tied to the banyan tree, the Sadhu performed the 'puja' most scrupulously and devoutly. After many days, the good and God-fearing Sadhu died. One of his chelas(disciple)- also a very conscientious and scrupulous man - took his place. He too, kept tying the cat to the sacred tree every time he performed his 'puja'. Unfortunately, some time later the cat died. The new Pujari was at a loss and perplexed. He kept asking himself: "Now that there is no cat, how can I possibly perform my 'puja'?" He thought and prayed about it. At last he found a solution. From that day on,

before the 'puja' would begin, you could have seen
the good and scrupulous Sadhu running down to the
nearest village street, catch any stray cat he could
find, take it to the temple, tie it to the banyan tree and
then only, scrupulously start his 'puja' in keeping with
all the customary rites and rubrics of the sacrifice"

"So you mean to say that, an authorizer doing
compliance checks is similar to the sadhu tying a
cat to the banyan tree," Mehul concludes
"I think we should assign this job to makers."
Pooja says.
"Wait ... When this process was started, I believe
there would have been some thinking gone into
this, based on which they would have decided
that this should be done by authorizers and not
makers," I comment
"What would it be?" Mehul asks. He is so impatient,
won't think for a second too, I wonder.
"Hmm ... May be risk," Mehul says.
"Risk ... Probably yes," I say and feel guilty of
quickly criticizing Mehul.
"So I guess we can't assign this task to makers,
and if we do and the makers miss out on any
compliance points we would be in a soup," Pooja
says.

"What if we reduce this risk?" Mehul asks.

"And how are we gonna do that?" Pooja asks.

"See the only risk you think, is what if the makers miss out... Right?" Mehul asks Pooja.

"Hmm … What point are you trying to make?" Pooja responds.

"Why would they miss?" Mehul asks and looks at me and winks. (he is trying to show off that, he is using the '5 Why's' principle).

"Because they are less experienced and not aware of all the points." She says.

"So if we train them on how to do compliance checks and if we introduce a compliance checklist with important points we check…" Mehul says, "I guess they would be as good as we are."

"Wow!! Good idea!! Where did he get this from?" I tell myself.

"Great idea!!" I say "moreover the chances of we missing out are also there, isn't it? …Your thoughts Pooja?"

"Sounds like a plan," Pooja says.

"Okay ..." I say and add in the 'I' column, "Pooja and Alban will take training on compliance checks today, and Mehul will create a checklist."

"So what next?" I ask.

"Monitoring team members." Mehul says.

"Hmm ... I remember Prof. Irani's words about monitoring team members from one of his lectures." I try to recollect as I say.

"What words??" Pooja asks.

"It goes like this … An employee telling his boss 'tell me how you gonna measure my performance, and I will tell you how I will perform'..." I say, "how do we measure their performance today?"

"Monthly … End of every month we send them the report of how many transactions each one has processed," Mehul says.

"Hmm… I think we should do it daily. Let us politely talk to the folks who are not performing," I say, "Moreover the authorizer's counts should be focused more on, as they are the bottlenecks"

"Hmm … I agree," Pooja says.

I notice Mehul is a bit confused, and I ask him "What happened? Are you not convinced?"

"No… I am convinced, just pondering on your professor's words" Mehul says.

"What?? …You don't agree?" I ask.

"NO… NO!! … I completely agree on that," he says, "but just wondering if the same applies for the team? And if yes, then why don't we measure team performance?"

There is silence now, it's a great point that he raised. If this holds good for an individual it should hold good for the team as well, I wonder.

"The objective of the team is to process transactions. That too in an agreed turnaround time and without errors," he says, "So I guess instead of an individual report card, we should send out the team's report card at regular intervals, which should include how many transactions we processed, with how many errors and how many TAT miss outs."

"Brilliant input … and it makes perfect sense … But we cannot exclude individual performances" I say.

"We can add individual performances also in this report." Mehul says.

"How??" I ask.

"We would show how much an individual has contributed in the team's performance e.g. Pooja contributes 10% whereas I might have contributed 12%" Mehul says.

"And how would we calculate that?" I ask.

"Don't worry about the calculations… Excel will take care of that." Mehul says.

"Calculation would be simple but what about the data? Who would collate it?" I ask, wondering that this might be extra work.

"See we have a system report which gives us count of the transactions, errors and TATs missed by individuals," Mehul says and continues, "Sum of individuals' scores would be the team score ...Right? ... Simple isn't it?" Mehul says.

"Hmm ... But I am still confused, on how you would use the data?" Pooja joins me.

"Hmm ..." Mehul wonders. He got it all right till now, but he is not sure how he would use these factors.

"It is simple Pooja," I come to Mehul's rescue.

"How??" Pooja asks, as Mehul gives me a startled look.

"Performance = more transactions, less error and less turn around time (TAT) issues," I say, "I will help Mehul in building this formula."

"That's fine... But what shall we compare the team report with?" Pooja questions.

"Good Question," I say, "start of every day, week and month we all (team) will decide a target."

"You mean to say we would set a daily target, a weekly target and a monthly target?"

"Yes ... Precisely and your report will compare the performance vis-a-vis the standards decided," I say.

"Excellent!!" Mehul says.

"I hope this works!!" Pooja says.

"It will…don't worry," I say and write it down in the 'I' column performance report.

"So what's next?" I ask again.

"Meetings … The most taxing part" Pooja obliges.

"I think the solution is simple here," I say, "we should avoid ad hoc meetings, and should have planned ones only. And most importantly we should have meetings post working hours."

They both agree and nod their heads, and I write 'meetings post working hours' in the 'I' column.

"Let's take monitoring workflow queue next" Mehul says enthusiastically before I could ask what next.

"Hmm … Why do we…??" I try to say something

"Wait… Wait!!" Mehul interrupts me and asks, "can I do this part?"

"Hmm … Ok." I say.

"So Al …why do we monitor workflow?" he tries to mimic me.

"Hmm … So that we ensure priority is followed," I say.

"Nothing is missed out," Pooja adds.

"Why do you think we have to ensure priority is to be followed and why do some transactions get missed out?" Mehul asks.

There is a silence. Pooja and I are wondering what the reason could be. It seems that Mehul knows the answer, but I guess he is trying to get it out from us.

"I think, we don't have an auto monitoring tool. Hence we have to manually do it, and sometimes it gets time consuming and is also error prone." Pooja says. Mehul smiles and I guess he was expecting this answer.

"Or it could be because we are responsible, since we are seniors, and that is expected out of us." I say. Mehul's smile disappears on hearing my reasoning.

"Ohh ...I didn't think about this" Mehul murmurs.

"What's on your mind Mehul?" I ask him.

"Actually, I felt that there must be a monitoring tool. However, a new application for doing that would involve a lot of cost and time. And right now I don't think we have either. Moreover, nobody is going to approve the cost of enhancement." Mehul says.

"So ...???" I ask.

"So ... I will create a macro enabled excel spreadsheet that updates the data from our workflow queues and sorts it based on the priority." He says.

"But how will that help?" I ask.

"It will …you have all the priority transactions on top and less priority down. Moreover, it will have a column, which will indicate how much time is left for the document to be processed vis-à-vis the Turn Around Time (TAT) agreed. So we would be saving almost 60 to 80 % of the authorizer's time here!" he says.

"That is fabulous," I say, "But with regards to the responsibility, I feel the makers should be made responsible on paper for monitoring transactions."

"We won't be monitoring anymore… that's what you are trying to convey?" Mehul tries to reconfirm his understanding

"Nopes, we would be, but not as frequently as we are doing now," I say, "Moreover this new macro enabled sheet would be a great aid." I update the 'I' column on the board with two points i.e. 'introduce the macro enabled priority sheet and assign responsibility of monitoring workflows to makers'.

"Hey, I think this priority sheet would take care of the assigning of jobs to makers also." Pooja says.

"Oh yeah … It would. We need not assign jobs anymore. The makers will pick up jobs based on the priority sheet" Mehul jumps in excitement "Why did I not realize it!"

"You need to have brains for that dumbo," Pooja comments.

"Great!!" I say and add it to the 'I' column.

"So what's left now?" I say knowing very well that the most time-consuming non-value adding activity i.e. Rework is left.

"REWORK…!!" Mehul shouts.

"This is a real pain." Pooja adds.

"So why do we have rework?" I ask.

"There are so many reasons, the list is exhaustive," Pooja remarks.

"Ok, let's work it out. As per Professor Irani, there is only one cause for all the problems" I say.

"So why do we have REWORK?" I ask again.

"Because, the inputters/makers are not processing the data correctly," Pooja says.

"And why are they not processing the data correctly, I mean, what is limiting them from doing so?" I ask.

"It is because they either do it hastily or maybe there is a knowledge gap," Pooja says.

"I don't think there is a knowledge gap here," Mehul says, "All of the makers are pretty seasoned now."

"Hmm … So why do they do transaction hastily?" I ask.

"They do it fast so that their count of transactions increases," Mehul adds.

"The top management always emphasizes on numbers and their year end performance is based on that," Pooja adds.

"Yeah, that's so very correct." I tell myself, and the email from Mr. Tendel comes in front of me. Everywhere there were numbers of transactions. Nowhere in the mail, was there a mention of errors.

"Yes you are correct, but how do we change the management's perception. It will always emphasize on volumes … numbers," Mehul says.

"I think we should explain to them with facts and figures, I see no reason why they should not believe this. Anyway, after our meeting today I am going to Mr. Tendel to take an approval, for name sake, on the changes we are going to put into effect... the 'I' column activities." I say.

"What the hell is this 'I' and 'other' column, why is this bifurcation?" Mehul finally blurts out his frustration.

"Hmm … This is something that I have learned over a period of time," I say.

"What is it??" Mehul asks.

"See … When you are effecting change, it should start with you. The process of the implementation would be faster." I say.

"I didn't get you?" Mehul says.

"Okay, let me tell you another story ... The Lark and his young ones." I say.

"Hey… I know that." Pooja shouts.

"Oh nice … do you want to narrate it?" I ask her

"Why not …" She responds, "The story goes like this …

A Lark made her nest in a field of wheat, which was just sown. As the days passed, the wheat stalks grew tall and the young birds, too, grew in strength. Then one day, when the ripe golden grain waved in the breeze, the farmer and his son came into the field. 'This wheat is now ready for reaping,' said the Farmer. 'We must call in our neighbors and friends to help us harvest it.'

The young larks in their nests close by were frightened, for they knew they would be in great trouble if they did not leave the nest before the reapers came. When the Mother Lark returned with food for them, they told her what they had heard.

'Do not be frightened, children,' said the Mother Lark. 'If the farmer said he would call in his neighbors and friends to help him do his work, this wheat will not be reaped for a while yet.'

A few days later, the wheat was so ripe, that when the wind shook the stalks, a hail of wheat grains came rustling down on the young larks' heads. 'If this wheat is not harvested at once,' said the Farmer, 'we shall lose half the crop. We cannot wait any longer for help from our friends. Tomorrow we must set to work, ourselves.'

When the young Larks told their mother what they had heard that day, she said:

'Then we must be off at once. When a man decides to do his own work and not depend on any one else, then you may be sure there will be no more delay.'

There was a lot of fluttering of wings that afternoon, and by sunrise next day, when the Farmer and his son cut down the grain, they found an empty nest."

"So what moral do we get from this" I ask and prefer to respond to it myself "Moral: Self-help is the best help. So the 'I' column would help us progress without any delays."

"Did you get it now?" Pooja asks Mehul in a sarcastic tone.

"Yes, I did," Mehul.

"Okay, so let me grab a cup of coffee and go to Mr. Tendel without further delay," I say and run to the canteen.

I quickly grab a cup of coffee and head straight to Mr. Tendel's cabin. On my way, Pooja and Mehul wish me good luck. I knock and enter the cabin.

"Good Morning Sir ... May I come in?" I say (don't know why I am asking this as I am already in).

"Ohh ... Good Morning Al!" he says, "Come in … Come in … Have a seat."

I sit down and give him a smile.

"What an artificial smile…!!" A thought pops up, "I should get the best artificial smile award or something"

"So tell me son ... What's the status?" Mr. Tendel interrupts my thoughts.

"Hmm…" before I could complete, he says "By status I mean … have you guys packed all your stuff, and everything is set to close down the process?"

I am a bit startled by this comment.

"I'm sorry sir, I did not get you!!" I say.

"What did you not understand… Alban!!!" he says, "We have only one month in hand of which already one week is gone. I've been observing your team all through the week, and you guys are having

159

meetings and meetings, but the performance over the last week has not improved a bit, in fact, it's deteriorated. The time spent in those unnecessary meetings would have helped in processing more transactions," he says.

"Sir those meetings ..." Again before I could complete, he interrupts and says.

"Enough of your meeting stuff, please go and authorize transactions. You are good for that only. I don't think you are capable of dealing with the situation. Anyway, I have called back Ajit, and he is expected to be here in a day or two" he says.

"But Sir... At least listen to me first!!" I plead.

"Alban, you can leave my cabin now, I have another call to attend." Mr. Tendel says.

The whole thing was very disturbing. I came out of the room not sure what to do. I try to hide myself from Pooja and Mehul and quickly go to the restroom. I go and sit on the commode and wonder... All the hard work we have put in has gone in vain. Two days later, Ajit would come and start doing things his ways, which would eventually shut the process. My thinking room was not helping me a bit today. "I lost it..." I say to myself, just then I could feel some vibration and wondered what happened. It was my cell phone, which was ringing, and Prof. Irani was calling.

"Prof Irani … at this time," I tell myself, as I answer the phone

"Hello," I say in a very low tone.

"Hello Al," Prof. Irani replied, "What's the matter with you?"

"Nothing sir," I say again in a low tone.

"Nothing … There is something wrong, what's the matter…? Is Bamboo theory not helping you?"

I break down and couldn't stop crying.

Prof. Irani lets me cry for a few minutes and then says, "Stop crying Al, because this is not going to help you in anyway. And now tell me what happened."

I tell him everything from identifying the bottleneck, brainstorming sessions with the team, subordination of task, to Mr. Tendel telling me I am incapable, and he has asked Ajit to join in.

"So when is Ajit coming back?" Prof. Irani asked.

"Maybe in a day or two," I replied.

"Okay … don't worry, you have got two days and you can still make an impact," Prof said.

"In two days, how is that possible?" I say.

"Don't you worry, just go ahead and implement the ideas right away." He says.

"But Mr. Tendel has not approved it yet," I say.

"Al … There is no time for approval!!!" Prof replied, "You want to save the process right?"

"Yes sir … I want to," I say.

"Don't worry, trust me and my Bamboo☺," He laughingly replies, "Everything would be okay … God bless you." And he disconnects

"Will god really bless me?" a thought pops up

CHAPTER 13

Break the Bottleneck

I come out, and both Pooja and Mehul are very eager to know what happened.

"What happened Alban?" Pooja asks

"Mr. Tendel has given the approval for implementing our ideas," I lie.

"That's excellent … let's inform the team about the changes then," Pooja says.

We inform the team about the changes. The team starts to work as per the new process now. For the first few hours, there is some confusion, nothing to worry though … it was due to some communication gap. Sometime later, the situation is under control. Transactions were moving faster than before. By EOD (end of the day) there is only two-day backlog instead of four days.

We all can see and feel that there is a difference. The process was more efficient now, however, I still wanted to wait and see if this behavior is consistent and not just a fluke

Next day, I come to the office all charged up. The staff was also charged up because of the volumes processed yesterday … Throughput rather. But before I could start authorizing transactions I receive a call from Ajit.

"Non-value add activity," I murmur and answer the call, "Hey Ajit"

"Hey Alban, how are you bro and how are things?" Bastard knows everything, still rubs salt to the wound.

"Everything is fine," I say.

"So what all improvements have you applied in the process so far," Ajit asks.

"Ohh … Seems like Ajit is really concerned about us… I am so bad that I mistook his intentions," I self criticize.

For the next 30 minutes, I explain him everything, and he listens to everything patiently.

"Thanks Alban, I am proud of you," He says with lots of emotion, "You have saved the process."

"Thanks Ajit for recognizing our efforts," I say.

"Chalo, Take Care… See you in a week's time".

"What did you say … One week or one day?" I try to confirm, as Mr. Tendel told me that he would be joining today.

"Yeah… one week later," he confirms

"Ohh … I thought you are coming tomorrow," I tell him.

"I was supposed to, but my mother in law wants me to stay for one more week," he says

"Probably… First time, somebody got a benefit out of a mother-in-law☺" I say to myself and smile.

"Ok, take care … See you when you are back," and I hang up.

I get back to work, as the time lost by the authorizer would mean loss in throughput. As I authorize the transactions, I can feel a different environment on the floor, it is no longer gloomy.

As I see my watch (it shows 6 PM), I wonder if we have improved our throughput—my gut feeling says "Yes"

"Hey Alban, good news," Mehul seconds my thought

"What is it?" I still ask, knowing the answer—throughput has increased.

"I proposed Rochelle and she said YES" Mehul winks

"What the F#&K," I shout and look at Rochelle (who is busy in her work).

"Why is it upsetting you... aren't you hitting on HJ?" Mehul asks me. As I stare him, I imagine having his lips in one hand and the big in my other hand, and Mehul is pleading "Please... Please don't staple my lips ...please"

"Dude... chill ... and stop staring at me," Mehul interrupts my imagination, "Neither am I HJ or Rochelle, nor have I proposed to Rochelle ... so chill"

"Asshole raised to infinity (Asshole^n) ... that's what you are," I say and smile.

"It was a conversation starter dude," and we both laugh.

"So, is there a real good news?" I try to bring us back to work

"Indeed ... We have reduced the backlog to one day, now" and we enjoy the moment.

Two great news— Ajit is delayed by a week, so I have got some more time to prove myself. And we are progressing well, and at this rate we would turn around the process in less than a week.

For next few days we work in a similar fashion, however, I am not getting the feeling that we are improving on the throughput. I send a meeting invite to Mehul and Pooja after the work hours.

We all gather at the agreed time.

"What's the matter Alban," Pooja asks, "Something wrong?"

"I have a feeling that, our throughput is not improving further," I respond

"Mehul … What does your number suggest," Pooja asks.

"Hmm … Yup, it has stabilized now. The first day we bought our backlog down from 4 to 2 days, next day it was down to 1 day, the day after it increased to 1.5 and today it is 1.35"

"Hmm … Now what next," Pooja asks.

"Let's call the professor," I recommend, they both nod in agreement and I dial the number.

"Hello, Prof Irani here"

"Sir Alban…"

"Yes Al … Tell me, what made you call me today … am sure you are stuck," he says

"Yes sir, we are kinda stuck," I tell him

"Go ahead … tell me the problem"

"As you suggested, we identified the bottleneck, exploited the bottleneck to the fullest, subordinated the non-value tasks to the non-bottlenecks," I try to build the problem

"Ok ... So what is the problem?"

"Sir, the throughput has stabilized and we still have a 1.5 day worth backlog to complete... How else can we increase the throughput?" I say

"Elevate the performance of bottleneck?" he says

"How ... can you be more specific? And what do you mean by elevate?" I ask.

"Elevate means ... Improve, promote, enhance the bottleneck," he says, "In this step, more substantive changes are implemented to 'break' the bottleneck. These changes may necessitate a significant investment of time and/or money (e.g. adding equipment or hiring more staff). The key is to ensure that all such investments are evaluated for effectiveness"

"Ok ..." I say, as I try to digest what the professor just said.

"Your team is very smart, and I am sure you will figure out a way to break the bottleneck... take care bye"

"Why is your professor always in a rush," Mehul asks.

"He might be a bottleneck somewhere," Pooja cracks a silly joke and we all laugh.

"So let us try to break the bottleneck," and I write this objective on the white board.

"Hire new staff i.e. authorizers," Mehul says, "That is the only way we can elevate the performance of the bottleneck"

"Hmm ... I think you are right," Pooja says

"I agree ..." I say remembering Mr. Tendel's words on new staff "But hiring new staff is out of question, we can't do that"

"Can we ask for help from other teams," Pooja suggests

"I think that is a good idea ... But not going to help us in the long run," I say, "but we can try that as a short term measure."

"Yeah, true ...we need to be self reliant," Pooja says.

"I got an IDEA," Mehul shouts, "Can we give authorization rights to some senior makers?"

"Wasn't that Ray's idea," Pooja counters.

"Yeah ... yeah ... whatever," he brushes off her comments

"Great IDEA though," Pooja joins him.

"Yeah, but there is a problem," I say

"What is it?" Mehul asks

"I don't have rights to give him authorizer entitlements, we need to go to Ajit or Mr. Tendel," I say, "Ajit is not here, and I don't think Mr. Tendel would give anybody authorizer entitlements based on my recommendations."

"Why? You explained him what we did right?" Mehul asks in a confused tone.

"I went to explain him, but he did not listen to me at all," I confess and tell them what happened.

"So the changes we have implemented are not approved by him?" Pooja asks

"Yes …" I say with some amount of guilt expecting a backlash from both of them.

"So can we do something similar here too?" she asks. I am surprised by her question, as she is not the one who takes risks.

"What worse can happen?" she continues with a smile, "you are anyway going to be sacked, for your wrongdoings… and not us ☺"

"Ok … Even if I agree to do this, how are we going to do it?" I smile and ask

"Dude, when Ajit went on leave he delegated all his tasks to you … Remember his OOO email," Mehul says.

"So you have the power of attorney," Pooja tries to provide an analogy.

"Yeah … You guys are right," I say, "Though operationally, I am not allowed to approve it. But in the system, I have the right to approve."

We decided unanimously that Ray would be given the entitlements to authorize, and discreetly, I give Ray those entitlements in the system.

Next day, we inform Ray about his new role and he was visibly very happy about it. Mehul comes close to me and scares me, "Hope in excitement he does not go and tell this to Mr. Tendel."

Giving Ray entitlements to authorize was showing effect, and the backlog was reducing significantly. At the end of the day we had around half a day's worth backlog and I was hopeful that tomorrow it would be reduced to zero.

Next day, I reach office very late and as I enter, I see Ajit's car parked outside the building. I ignore it assuming that it would be somebody else's car with the same model. As I reach the floor, I see Ajit on his desk, and I say to myself "What the F#$K is he doing here today". Ajit waves his hands and calls me to his desk. I go to him with a predetermined thought that I would not tell him about the latest changes and that we would shortly turnaround the process. I go to his desk and for about an hour he spoke about everything else apart from work. He spoke about his journey, his honeymoon blah…. blah… blah…!!

I come back to my desk after wasting an hour and wondered how much it would have affected our throughput. It was around lunchtime, when Mehul comes to my desk and shouts.

"Alban … We have created HISTORY !! We have created HISTORY !!

"What happened dude?? Why are you shouting?" I ask him gesturing to cool down.

"There are zero transactions in queue," He says, "We have cleared them all."

"Are you sure?" I ask in disbelief, "There might be some problem with the workflow system."

"No … No problem," He said, "I had called up the branch manager also, and she confirmed there are no transactions. She sounded very happy today."

"This would be for the first time that we have cleared all the WON (work order numbers)," he adds

"I am so happy," I say, "Bamboo Theory actually worked… it ACTUALLY WORKED!!!"

"Yes it had to," Pooja adds and joins in our celebrations

"Has the number of documents scanned reduced?" I am still skeptical.

"Nopes ... in fact they were higher than the average," Mehul says.

"Cool ... let's celebrate ... Pizza treat on me tomorrow," I say. I try to call Prof Irani, to thank him, but he does not answer my call. Nevertheless, I thank him for these beautiful insights called *"Bamboo* Theory"

CHAPTER 14

Final Showdown

While we were celebrating, Ajit gets a call, and he rushes to Mr. Tendel's office. After 15 minutes he comes out, with a big smile on his face.

"What happened Ajit? … You seem to be very happy," I ask.

"Yeah … Singapore branch manager has praised our efforts, and they are very happy with me being back," Ajit says.

"What!!" I am startled.

"I'm kidding … They are happy because we have cleared the queues," He says.

Before I could say anything, Rakesh (AVP from another team) comes and congratulates Ajit.

"Good show Ajit, well done," Rakesh says.

"What happened?" Mehul enquires.

"Go check your mails," Rakesh says. We all go to our respective desks and check our mails. It was Mr. Tendel's appreciation email copied to the whole department which stated,

Dear Team

Just want to share with you a success story. It is a story of a team, which was in deep shit for quite some time now. I am sure you all would be aware (from grapevine sources) that Singapore Branch had decided to take back the documentation process due to poor service delivery. They had given us only a month's notice for improvement. To add on to our problems, Ajit was getting married and was not available. I had no choice but to grant him his leave.

On the floor, things were deteriorating day by day. Others in the team tried their best (at least that's what they claim) but all in vain. I was left with no choice but to call back Ajit from his leave.

On my special request, Ajit was back and in a day he has turned it around. The process has streamlined now. I have never seen an email from Singapore Branch manager praising any of our process improvements. In this case, they personally called to acknowledge the hard work we have done.

It would not have been possible without Ajit.

Dear Ajit

Thanks for the sacrifice you made on your personal front for this crisis we are in, and I am really proud of you

Regards
R. Tendel
VP - Operations

"Too much!!!" I shouted. Ajit heard that and looked at me. He knew it very well that, I had done all the hard work, and he just came and took away all the credit. I could no longer take it, and I headed straight to Mr. Tendel's office. I barged into his cabin and in a very stern tone said, "Sir I want to talk … now … And it's pretty urgent."

He was startled to see this reaction, but calmly said, "I'll call you back in sometime," and he hung up the phone.

"I knew you would come, I expected you to come," he said. Now, I was a bit startled with this comment.

"Me and my team have done all the hard work, and Ajit takes all the credit," I say, "How is this fair?"

"Do you think I don't understand what is happening in my team?" Mr. Tendel replied.

"Then why this appreciation email to Ajit?" I asked.

"I did that on purpose ... I had a word with Ajit this afternoon, and I could gauge that he had no clue on what was happening in the team."

"Hmm... But why that appreciation to Ajit?" I asked.

"I was doing my job son ... I was checking on the integrity of my subordinates," He replied. "But I am still not very sure, if what your team has achieved is just a fluke or it is actually a process change."

"Sir ... for the last entire week me and my team have been trying to diagnose the cause for this problem we are in and we have been successful in doing it. Based on the diagnosis we have come out with some solutions and changes, which we had to implement right away. And I had come the other day just to discuss it with you and implement it," I say, "But you were not even ready to listen to me and threw me out of your cabin. That left me with no choice but to effect the changes without your approvals"

There is silence—I was wondering whether I spoke too much. Don't know what Mr. Tendel would be thinking now, but he seemed to be lost in deep thought.

"Hmm … Forget what happened. Now tell me how all this started?" He says.

"Hmm … Ok …to start with, after receiving your email about overstaff capacity I was wondering that there is something amiss here—either with the way we process or the way capacity is measured."

"So what was the conclusion?" Mr. Tendel enquired.

"Eventually both were, and that was the starting point of diagnosing the problem," I say.

"My way of measuring was not wrong Alban, that's the way how Industry measures capacity, that's the way how staffing is made, etc." Mr. Tendel says.

"Sir … If you give me some time, I'll explain and prove you wrong," I confidently say.

"Go ahead … All the best," He says.

"First, we identified the goal of the company, the purpose why this process was formed and related it to our job," I say.

"And what is it?" Mr. Tendel enquired.

"It is to make money… now … and in future," I say and wait for some time for him to digest this fact. I could see on his face that he was trying to verify this goal with one of those generally accepted goals i.e. maximizing profits, reducing cost, etc.

"Hmm … This is very short and crisp," Mr. Tendel replied and now he was a bit more involved in the discussion.

"Yeah, it is sir, I'm sure it covers all the definitions you had in mind," I say.

"Yeah … It does, but you need to get all the members in the team aware of this," Mr. Tendel smilingly says.

"Yes, we have to and that was the first item on our to do list," I said

"Ok … So what's next?" he enquires.

"We then derived a formula to attain this goal," I replied.

"Oh…formula and all!!" Mr. Tendel comments.

"Yes … and we had related it to our daily work. In short, we have related the daily work we do to the goal."

"Hmm … Good, but can you explain to me in detail."

"Yes the formula includes three components, measurements or whatever you call it i.e. Throughput, Operational Expenses and inventory," I say and brief him on the definitions.

"So to achieve the goal, we need to increase the throughput first and then decrease Operational Expenses and Inventory." I say.

"All along, we have been focusing on decreasing operational expenses only," Mr. Tendel comments.

"Yes sir, that is precisely right and we have come up with several solutions."

"You mean to say increase Throughput right?" he asks.

"Correct …"

"So what's next?" he enquires.

"Sir the next thing we did was identifying the process constraint… the BOOCH," I respond

"Process bottleneck… BOOCH??" Mr. Tendel asked in a surprised tone.

"Yes sir BOOCH, and this is what helps us increase the throughput, and also would help me in proving that your calculation on capacity was wrong," I reply.

"Ok … Go ahead."

"Now that you are aware of throughput, which is nothing but the number of docs we process correctly… Can I safely assume, that you agree that capacity of the process can also be referred to as throughput of the system?" I ask and he gestures his agreement

I take out a blank sheet from my file and describe him and draw a high-level process map.

Customer–>Scanning–>Inputting–>Authorizing

"This is our high level process map… Customer presents the documents at the branch counters, scanners at the branches scan and send the same to us, and makers input the documents into the system, and finally authorizers authorize the transactions … Correct sir?" I ask.

"Ok …" Mr. Tendel says and nods.

"So let me assign the current capacity to these activities." I say.

"Go ahead."

After assigning the capacity the map looks like below:

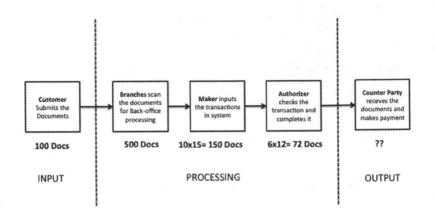

"What is this 10 x 15 and 6 x 12?" Mr. Tendel asked. "Sir, there are 10 makers and the average number of docs processed by the maker is 15, so the capacity of Makers is 10 x 15 docs = 150 docs, similarly for the Authorizers." I replied.

"Hmm ... So, what are you trying to conclude?" Mr Tendel asks looking at the Question marks in the diagram

"From this I conclude two things, first that the bottleneck is the authorizer, and second, the capacity of the whole process is only 72 docs and not 128 docs as mentioned in your email," I say.

Mr. Tendel again goes into a thinking mode and after a few minutes, he replies,

"Yes, you are right and I was wrong. Each document before processing goes through each of this processes and the lowest capacity of the process would determine the capacity of the entire process." Mr Tendel responds

"That's absolutely correct sir," I say, "Moreover our capacity is much lower than 72."

"How is that?" Mr. Tendel asks.

"Ajit is one of those six authorizers and he hardly checks any documents. So if I minus him, our capacity (Throughput) would be 60 documents only. And customer presents us 100 docs a day, and that's why the work is getting piled up by each passing day," I say.

"Hmm ... So you have identified and implemented ways of increasing capacity of the authorizers?" Mr. Tendel asks.

"Yes Sir ... that's correct." I say.

"Briefly, tell me how have you done it?" Mr. Tendel asks

"Sir firstly, we have to ensure that the bottleneck i.e. authorizers are fully exploited. Any waste of time by them is a reduction of throughput of the system. The same was conveyed to them, and they understood it well." I replied.

"Next, we tried to pass on non-value adding activities done by authorizers to the makers, since they were excess capacity. This way the number of transactions authorized by the checkers/authorizers increased considerably."

"How?" Mr. Tendel asked.

"Sir … because of the delegation to makers and other improvements, the time taken by the authorizers for processing one transaction reduced from 30 to 18 minutes. Thus, the capacity increased from 60 to 100 docs. (12 docs x 30mins/18mins x 5 authorizers)"

"But then maker's capacity would have reduced?" Mr. Tendel enquired.

"Yes, it did but the authorizers are still bottlenecks." I say.

"How?" he asked.

"Sir, their processing time increased from 30 minutes to 40 minutes, thus the capacity decreased from 150 docs to 112 docs (15 docs x 30mins/40mins x 10) makers)." I say, "So reduced capacity of maker (112) is still more than increased capacity of authorizers (100)"

"Also, I gave Ray entitlements to Authorize, without your permission," I say, and wait for Mr. Tendel to react. He just throws a poker face at me and I continue, "We use him as a joker card, that is, he assumes a role based on the bottleneck at that point in time"

"Good idea," He said, "No wonder how you all have managed to zero down the workflow queues ... Great job."

He then calls up his secretary, "Rosy .... Hi ... Please ask Ajit to come to my office immediately."

"Now what is he up to?" Thought pops up.

In a few minutes, Ajit enters the room with a big smile on his face. Seeing my smile his smile disappears.

"Hi Ajit ... I have some news for you." Mr. Tendel says.

"Yes ... sir ... What is it?" Ajit asks.

"From today ... Alban will take over your role of Head of Documentation Team," Mr. Tendel says.

Ajit and I, both are in a state of shock and surprised with the turn of events. I thank Prof Irani for this beautiful insight... *Bamboo* Theory, and wonder what is in store for Ajit ... Keep guessing ... No prizes for guessing what happened to Ajit ☺

Printed in the United States
By Bookmasters